The Sixth Book of Moses called GOOD GOVERNMENT!

(The Primary Missing Book in the Holy Bible!)

By
The Worldwide People's Revolution!®

♦♦ Book 126 ♦♦

(The Cover Photo shows a Malachite Pyramid, which is Representative of the Kingdom or Government of God, with the Most-High God Moklom at the very Top of it! And that, my Friend, is your First Test of Faith. So, Hang in there: beCause it gets Really Good, later! Guaranteed!)

Copyright, Dedication and Introduction

♦♦♦♦♦♦♦ By our Selected King's Chief Editor — Dr. Samuel Walker Edison — Ph.D., M.A., BS and QC!

ISBN — 979-8669-7817-67

00-01 [_] This Inspired Book is COPYRIGHTED AD 2020, by **The Worldwide People's Revolution!®** All Rights are Reserved for Moses' Sake, who was Unjustly Mistreated by the Deletion of his Sixth Book, called: **"Good Government,"** which contained far too many Provable Truths for the Lying Conniving Edomites to Deal with: beCause they were (and still are) Possession Worshipers, who were called *Baal Worshipers* during Ancient Times, who took Full Advantage of that Thing called MONEY, whereby they might make themselves Excessively Rich; but, it was not the Will of God, nor of Moses, Joshua, Elijah, Samuel, King David, Isaiah, Jeremiah, Ezekiel, Daniel, Hosea, Amos, Joel, Jonah, Malachi, Jesus, John, Peter, James, the Apostle Paul, nor of any of the other Holy Prophets and Apostles: beCause, they all Believed in GOOD Government, which is a Pyramid Kingdom, with the Greatest King at the very Top of it, who is Naturally the Great Creator God, or Most-High God, who Created all Living Things in a Great Multitude of Universes, each of which Contain a Great Multitude of Galaxies, each of which Contain a Great Multitude of Solar Systems with Nebulas, Stars, Planets, Earths, Moons, Comets, Asteroids, and other Heavenly Bodies, which Solar Systems are Inhabited with Various Kinds of People, most of whom Liv on the Insides of the Planets, from which their Moons were Born: beCause they are Hollow, even as this Earth is Hollow, from which our Moon was Born, which is also Inhabited with Great Multitudes of People, including Various Kinds of GIANTS, plus the Holy City of the Supreme Ruler of this World of Wonders, called Mount Zion, which is a Great Plateau, which is about 1 Mile High, 200 Miles (322 Kilometers) Long and 100 Miles Wide, which is Surrounded by a Deep Gorge, or Ravine, through which the Surrounding Tall Mountains are Drained, which Converge at the Northern-most Point, to form the Mighty Jordan River, which Drains into the Arctic Sea, which also Forms Great Icebergs, when the Jordan River is Frozen each Winter, at the Northern-most End of it, which Causes the Water to be BACKED-UP a Mile or so Deep, which Forms a Great DAM by the Ice, which is under Tremendous PRESSURE from the Backed-up Water, which Pushes the Iceberg into the Arctic Sea when Summer comes and Melts enough Ice to Release the Iceberg, which is Locked between 2 Great Mountains, called Moklom and Keeoojum, being Named after the Supreme Ruler of this Galaxy, and the Supreme Ruler of this Universe, who is Keeoojum, who is the Most-High God of this Vast Universe, which is only One of Multitudes of Universes like this, which are Invisible to us: beCause of being too Far Away!

00-02 [_] No Portion of this Inspired Book shall be Reproduced by any Means for Sale without Written Permission from "The Worldwide People's Revolution!" (A Comprehensive Plan for Obtaining Worldwide Law, Order, Obedience, Peace and True Prosperity!) By The Worldwide People's Revolution!® Book 108: beCause, our Selected King Wants 10% of the Net Profits for the Construction of: "The Great World TEMPLE of PEACE!" (The Glory of Jerusalem Arises Again in the Great State of Flexible Texas!) By The Worldwide People's Revolution!® Book 017B, which will be the HEADQUARTERS for: "The New RIGHTEOUS One-World Government!" (HOW to Establish a Righteous One-World Government without Going to WAR!) By The Worldwide People's Revolution!® Book 056, which will be in the Midst of "A New Jerusalem in the Great State of Flexible Texas!" (HOW to make Good Use of the Mississippi River!) By The Worldwide People's Revolution!® Book 090, which will be about 100 Miles in Diameter, being Built Up in Great Stone TERRACES, in Order to Form a Mighty Swanky FORTRESS! (*Swanky* Means *First-Class Quality* throughout all Swanky Literature, which consists of more than 364 Inspired Books, or one for each Day of the Year, which is made up of 13 Months, with 28 Days in each Month, or Exactly 4 Weeks in each Month, with a Leap-Week once every 28 Years, and another Leap-Week whenever it is Needed, in Order to have a Permanent Calendar with 28 Days in each Month, which should be made of Brass or Bronze. †‡)

00-03 [_] O Doctor Samuel Walker Edison, what shall the other 90% of the Money be Used for, from the Sales of this Most-Astounding New Book, which will be Number One on the Market? †§

00-04 [_] Well, my Friend, that Money may be Used by the Person, Organization or Company, who Sells the Book for a Reasonable Profit, as well as any of the 125 other Inspired Books, which are Listed in Chapter 40, which Deal with Various Important Subjects, for Wise People to Study.‡

00-05 [_] So, O Dr. Sam, what is the Reason for Obtaining Written Permission from "The Worldwide People's Revolution!" just to Sell the Books? Can I not be Trusted to do my Tithing?

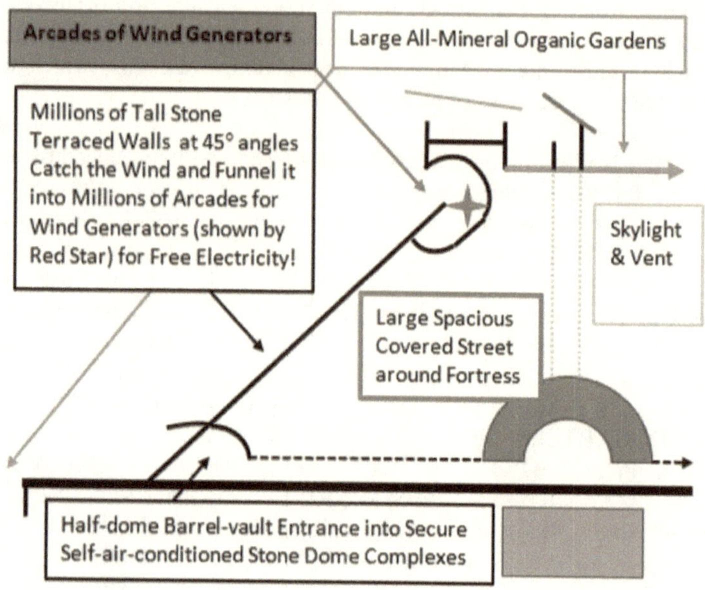

00-06 [_] Well, my Friend, the Reason is to Prevent any Cheating, and to make Sure that our Selected King gets 10% of the Net Profits for the Construction of "The Great World TEMPLE of PEACE!" which will be the Tallest and Largest Building in the Whole World, which will be Built Up in 60 Great Stone Terraces: beCause, each Terrace will Contain thousands of those "Beautiful Swanky Stone Dome Home COMPLEXES!" (HOW to Build SECURE Tax-proof, Insurance-proof, Self-air-conditioned, Paint-proof, Rot-proof, Termite-proof, Mouse-proof, Fireproof, Tornado-proof, Hurricane-proof, Thief-proof, and BOMB-PROOF Houses!) By The Worldwide People's Revolution!® Book 102, which will be Occupied by the Elected Officials of "The New RIGHTEOUS One-World Government!" who will get up and go to Work in the Great Throne Room, which will have Special Seats and Desks for 6 High Priests, who will Represent all Major and Minor Religious Groups — such as Christians, Muslims, Hindus, Buddhists, Mormons, Jehovah's Witnesses, and so on — plus Special Seats and Desks for 60 Elected Kings from 60 Major Nations, plus a Maximum of 600 Special Seats and Desks for a Maximum of 600 Elected

Governors from Minor Nations, Provinces, and Islands of the Seas. In other Words, none of those Leaders will have any Sorry Excuses for not Working 6 Days per Week, according to the Laws of Moses, which were not Done Away with: beCause, they must be Fulfilled, which Means that the Sabbath Day is still the Seventh Day of the Week, even as it was the Lord's Day of Rest ever since the Beginning, when he Created the Countless Heavens and Earths, and everything within the Vast Multitudes of Galaxies in this Universe, SPIRITUALLY, within only 6 Days, and Rested during the Seventh Day. In other Words, he *Planned* it all within just 6 Days: beCause, that is what a Marvelous Mind that the Great Creator God has, who is otherwise called The Most-High GOD: beCause, *God* Means *The Supreme Ruling Family of Holy Ones, who have been Perfected in the Furnace of Afflictions:* beCause, each of the Gods must be TESTED for their Goodness, just to Qualify as Supreme Rulers of their own Worlds, even as Jesus Christ was Tested by Various Temptations, to Qualify as the Supreme Ruler of this World, which was Created According to his Desires: beCause, he was Found Worthy to Inherit such a World: beCause of Passing his Tests in other Worlds, who became the Creator of this World, you might say, in the Sense that it was Created According to his Desires, by the Great Creator God, who is the Invisible God, whom no Man has ever Seen: beCause he is a Great SPIRIT Being, who Livz everywhere, who is the SUPREME RULER of all Supreme Rulers, who are called GODS: beCause, each of the Worlds Requires a God to Govern it, even as each of the Solar Systems Requires a God to Govern it. For Example, the Supreme Ruler of this Solar System is JEHOVAH God, Yahweh God, or YHWH God, who Chose the Tribe of ISRAEL to Govern this World: beCause they are the Better Spirits, whose First Father was called ADAM, who was the Beginning of the Creation of Yohoovu God in this World, which was already Inhabited by Black and Brown Peoples from other Worlds, who were Transported over here from those other Worlds by the GIANTS, who had Great Spaceships, even as they still have within the Hollow Earth, who can Travel between the Various Worlds, including the Most-Beautiful World of all in this Solar System, which is JUPITER, which is the Headquarters for Yohoovu God, who Livz in the Inner-most World within that World, which is made of Concentric Worlds within Worlds: beCause, each of those Worlds is HOLLOW! In other Words, it is like a Basketball within a Basketball, whereby each Basketball gets smaller and smaller, which are Inhabited on the Insides and Outsides of them: beCause, Jupiter is the Perfect PARADISE in this Solar System; and Yohoovu God Livz in the Most-Perfect Paradise in the Central World, being Attended to by his Holy Angels, most of whom are also GIANTS with Great Wings, Long Blond Hairs, Blue Eyes, and White Skins, even as Adam was, whom

Yohoovu God Created to Govern this World, who was the First White Man, like us, in this World, who brought about the Fall of Mankind by Eating the Forbidden Fruit from the Tree that Represented the NOLIJ of ALL that is GOOD and EVIL: beCause of Yielding to the Will of his Wife, called Mother EVE, who Yielded to the Temptation of Satan, the Devil, who Appeared to her as a Talking Snake, even though he is also a Great SPIRIT BEING, who Livz Everywhere in this Order of Worlds, in Order to Tempt People to SIN, which is a Transgression of God's Laws. Therefore, when Adam Ate the Forbidden Fruit, which Represented the Nolij of All that is Good and Evil, he was Cast Out of the Paradise of Peace and Happiness, which is on the Inside of this Good Earth, which has no Night: beCause, it has its own Central Light, which will be Replaced during the Future by the New Jerusalem, which will be Coming Down from the Sky, from Jupiter, when Yohoovu God Discovers that we are Worthy of it, after we have Constructed "The Great World TEMPLE of PEACE!" in the Great State of Flexible Texas for The KING of Kings and his Good Government, called: "The New RIGHTEOUS One-World Government!" which has more than "101 Good Reasons and Great Advantages for Establishing a Righteous One-World Government!" (Government By the People, Of the People, and For the People!) By The Worldwide People's Revolution!® Book 104. Yes, Adam was Cast Out of the Garden of Eden, which was Built by the Holy Angel, called EDEN, who is still in Charge of it, within the Hollow Earth: beCause, the TREE of LIFE did not Die, my Friend; but, it was Preserved for the Holy Ones, and Especially for the Anointed Savior, whom we call JESUS CHRIST, who Paid the Price for Committing the Original Sin in the Garden of Eden, by his Self-Sacrifice on a Torture Stake, Outside of Jerusalem, when he was Crucified by the Romans, who were Orchestrated by those Lying Conniving EDOMITES, who Objected to the Teachings of the Anointed Savior, who got to Reed **"The Sixth Book of Moses, called: GOOD GOVERNMENT!"** In Fact, it is still Preserved in Mount Zion, which is the Holy City of the Great King, which you can Reed about in *Psalm 48,* which is no Poetic Nonsense: beCause, it is a Real City, even a Mighty Swanky FORTRESS, with Tall Stone Walls surrounding it, and with Holy Angels Dancing on Top of that Great Wall, many of whom are 30 to 40 Feet Tall, and with Great Blond Wings, Blue Eyes, and Blond Hairs with Blond Skins, which are like the Young Man whose Photo appears in: "Good Lessons for Honest Wise Men!" (A Simplistic Plan for Totally Solving the Complicated Problems of Deceived Mankind!) **By The Smarter Professor of Common Sense!** Book 125. †‡

00-07 [_] O Doctor Samuel Walker Edison, I can hardly Believe my Eyeballs! Where did you get all such Inspired Words from? Are you Sure that it is Legal to Publish all such Provable Truths? ‡

00-08 [_] Well, my Friend, I got those Inspired Words from the Holy Spirit, even as our Selected King Wrote them, Years Ago, when he was Moved by the Holy Spirit to Write them: beCause, *All Scriptures are Given by the Inspiration of the Most-High God, and are Profitable for Teaching Good Doctrines, for Reproving Sinners, for Correcting Saints, and for Instructions in the Ways of Righteousness, whereby the Man of God might be Thoroughly Furnished with the Proper Tools for Constructing his own House of Love on the Solid Bedrock of Divine Truths, which no Violent Wind will Blow Away, nor will any Flood of Water Wash it Away, nor will any Fire Burn it Up: beCause of being Like one of those* "Beautiful Swanky Stone Dome Home COMPLEXES!" (HOW to Build SECURE Tax-proof, Insurance-proof, Self-air-conditioned, Paint-proof, Rot-proof, Termite-proof, Mouse-proof, Fireproof, Tornado-proof, Hurricane-proof, Thief-proof, and BOMB-PROOF Houses!) By The Worldwide People's Revolution!® Book 102. ‡

00-09 [_] O Doctor Sam, I must Confess that I have the Utmost Respect for the Holy Spirit, who alone could Inspire all such Beautiful Words; but, WHO is your Selected King, and WHY do we Need a RIGHTEOUS KING to Govern us? Will he be the Selected King for "The New RIGHTEOUS One-World Government!" (HOW to Establish a

Righteous One-World Government without Going to WAR!) By The Worldwide People's Revolution!® Book 056?

00-10 [_] Well, my Friend, our Selected King is the Man with the Spirit of Elijah, who has Come to Restore "Provable Truths that True Christians cannot Rightly Deny!" (A Fair Challenge for all Professing "Christians" to Meditate on with Honest Open Minds!) By The Worldwide People's Revolution!® Book 086, who is also the Inspired Author of: "The New MAGNIFIED Version of the Book of DEUTERONOMY!" (The Understandable Version of Deuteronomy in Plain English!) Book 084, which is a Companion Book of: "The Process of Making a RIGHTEOUS KING!" (A Fascinating Autobiography of our Selected King!) By The Worldwide People's Revolution!® Book 082, which is a Companion Book of: "Guaranteed Solutions!" (HOW to Solve our Local and Global Problems in the Most-Rational Manner Possible!) By The Worldwide People's Revolution!® Book 080, which is a Companion Book of: "The New MAGNIFIED Version of the HOLY KORAN!" (WHY MuhamMAD went to Hell for Spiritual MURDER!) By The Worldwide People's Revolution!® Book 089, which is a Companion Book of: "The New MAGNIFIED Version of The Book of MORMON!" (The Story of the White and Dark Indians in the Americas!) By Big Chief Standsover Bull in River of Life! Book 040, which is even more Awesome than this Inspired Book: beCause, it gets a 7-Diamond Rating, which is so Good that the Queen of England Awarded our Selected King with her own Golden Coach, which is Pictured on the Front Cover of that Amazingly Good Book! Therefore, this Inspired Book is now DEDICATED to Moses, who will Reed it and Realize that it is his Duty to Help the Man with the Spirit of Elijah to get the Household of Israel Corrected: beCause, they are Represented by the 2 Great Candlesticks and Olive Trees in *Revelation 11.* †§‡

{FOOTNOTE 01 — The Explanations for Symbols can be found in: "Which Church is the Right Church?" (Can all Churches be Correct?) **By The Good Pastor of Uncommon Sense!** Book 119, which will not Fry your Eyeballs to Study it; but, it might Change your Mind and Heart for "The Hopeless Church of Little Faith!" (The Unholy Church of Graceful Sinners, who are Mostly just Liars and Hypocrites!) **By The Good Pastor of Uncommon Sense!** Book 121!}

The Fascinating MENU on the Table of CONTENTS
for a Satisfying Feast of Probable Truths!

{HEADNOTE: This Inspired Book contains several Educational Photographs with Enlightening Explanations for Wise People to Study with Honest Open Minds, who have not gotten themselves Lost in the Darkness of Ignorance, along with about 40,000 Words that should have been Written in the *Holy Bible,* by Moses, Joshua, Samuel, Elijah, Daniel, King David, Isaiah, or whomever was Close to God and the Realities of Life. Therefore, do not Forget to Pass this Information on.}

{Missing Chapters will be Supplied when they are Demanded by the Readers!}

The Symbols (†§‡§§) are Carefully Explained in: "Which Church is the Right Church?" (Can all Churches be Correct?) By The Good Pastor of Uncommon Sense! Book 119, for which there are 5 Editions on Amazon.com, which have Free Book Previews for Diligent Wise Readers. For Example, there are Black and White Editions in 2 Sizes, and Colored Editions in 2 Sizes, which are more Expensive than the Black and White; but, for really Poor People, there is a KDP Electronic Edition for a Dollar or 2, which has Colored Pictures, which most People Prefer, unless they are Looking for Collector's Items, in which Case the 8.5 by 11-inch Colored Edition in the Paperback Format is Best: beCause it will be a LIMITED Edition: beCause of becoming Leather-bound with other Inspired Books, during the Future, when all such Books will Replace the *Unholy Mutilated Bible* with "An Amazing Collection of Wit and Wisdom!" (The Marvelous Tale of the Colorful Peacock from Angel Ridge, and the Strong Rope of Everlasting Hope!) By The Worldwide People's Revolution!® Book 048, which makes the Best Reading in the World! †§‡

WARNING: There are Screen Shots in this Edition of the Book, which might have Print that is too small to read with Comfort. Therefore, we Recommend the 8.5 by 11-inch Colored Edition, which also has Line Numbers and larger Photographs and Drawings, in most cases. (For some Unknown Reason, Amazon does not like to Sell it; but, you should Ask them for it, anyway. All of the Paragraphs are Justified at the Ends of the Lines, even as they were Inspired.) Moreover, all Recent Books come in 5 Editions of 2 different Sizes, one being an Electronic Edition (E-Book), which is the least Expensive; but, if you are looking for a Collector's Item, the above Recommended Colored Edition is Best. Furthermore, almost all of the Original Books have "Deliberate Minor Errors" in them, for making them more Valuable as Collector's Items: beCause, Future Editions will have those Errors Corrected. Therefore, if you can Afford it, now is the Time to get yourself at least one Copy of this Inspired Book, and keep it in Good Condition, which is in a Unique Class of its own, being Very Special, being one of the Master Farmer's Favorite Books! ENJOY!

♦ — Chapter 01 — ♦

Moses Introduces himself!

01-01 [_] Now, O Readers, you might be Surprised to Learn that I am still Alive and Well, who Appeared with Elijah and the Glorified Savior on the Mount called Transfiguration, along with Peter, James and John, who were more than Amazed by the Giant Size of Jesus Christ in his Glorified State, who was about 40 Feet Tall, and Plenty Large enough to have Won any Wrestling Match with any Man on this Good Earth, including Abraham Lincoln, who also Liked to Wrestle Naked, even as I Wrestled Naked with Yohoovu God at the Brook called Penuel, which you can Read all about in *Genesis 32,* which clearly states that I Prevailed in that Wrestling Match, in Verse 28, King James Version (KJV), which is the one and only Reliable Translation among 200-plus Versions: beCause, it uses Elizabethan English, which was not even Invented until about AD 1611. Indeed, you must Understand that I am being very Sarcastic about that: beCause, there is no Way on this Good Earth that a Translation of *Ancient Scriptures* could be Correct, if it were not a Perfect Translation of those Chicken Scratches, you might say, called HEBREW, which was written Upside Down, from the Bottom of the Paper to the Top of it, and from the Right Side of the Paper to the Left Side: beCause, it was Invented by a Left-Handed Man called Joojubee, who Lived at the Time of Adam, who was Tawt how to Reed and Riit in Swanky Funetik English, using Roman Letters, if you can Believe it. However, I am only being Sarcastic, once again: beCause, I Like to Force People to THINK, which most People do not Like to Do: beCause they only like to DREAM!

01-02 [_] O Moses, are you going to be so Kind as to Answer all of our Important Questions; or, will we have to Rely on the Man with the Spirit of Elijah to get everything just Riit, since he seems to be Gifted with RIGHTEOUSNESS, which is something that the Present-day Politicians in Washington, District of Chief Criminals, seem to Know nothing about, who do not even Capitalize LOVE nor HATE: beCause, they are Filled with the Unholy Spirit of IGNORANCE and Stupidity!

01-03 [_] Well, my Friend, I have no Idea what I will Riit: beCause, like all of the Holy Prophets, I will simply Rely on the Holy Spirit, and Trust her to get it Riit, who is a Near Relative of Wisdom, as King Solomon Explained in: **"The ACTS of KING SOLOMON, First and Last,"** who was not so Wise as he should have been: beCause, he made the Big Mistake of Building a WOODEN Temple, which the Babylonians Burned Down; but, it will not be the Case for **"The Great World TEMPLE of PEACE!" (The Glory of Jerusalem Arises Again in the Great State of Flexible Texas!) By The Worldwide People's Revolution!® Book 017B:** beCause, it will all be Built of Fireproof Materials — such as Polished Stones on Solid Rock and Concrete Walls, even as our Selected King Constructed his 100,000-gallon Cistern for Water Storage, for Watering his All-Mineral Organic Garden, after **"Seven Great Armies of Working Soldiers!" (HOW to Provide a Way for Everyone to WORK: so as to Eliminate Poverty, Crimes, Drug Abuses, Prisons and Unnecessary Taxes!) By The Worldwide People's Revolution!® Book 015B,** got 180,000 Wheelbarrows of Dirt SIFTED, by Hand, whereby they Removed no less than 60,000 Wheelbarrows of Small Rocks, just to Exaggerate Things a bit, whereby you might Relate with the Difficult WORK that was Required for Building such a Garden, according to: **"The LUSCIOUS All-Mineral Organic Method of Gardening!" (HOW to Grow DELICIOUS Satisfying Foods for Potential Kingz and Kweenz in Beautiful Swanky PALACES!) By The Worldwide People's Revolution!®** Book 021B, which you are Welcome to MOCK, if ye Wants to, along with that Poor Nigger Jim and his Imprisoned Tax Slave called Huck Finn, who never got around to Reading: "Modern Deceived SLAVES!" (10 Simple Steps for Liberating ALL Modern Slaves, Worldwide, Including Yourself!) **By Liberty and Justice for ALL!** Book 113: beCause of being far too Busy Playing with his Little Balls and Tally Whacker: beCause, he was Born to be a SERVANT, and not a Master, like me, nor like our Selected King, who also likes to Exaggerate Things, just to make certain Points of Interest more Interesting for his Readers. †§‡§§

01-04 |_| After all, you must Realize that most People have Drugged Minds, which are not Functioning very Well, like that of the Brilliant Mind of Professor Arnold Ehret, who could Speak 7 Languages Fluently, while I do Well to Speak just ONE: beCause it is only Necessary to Speak one Language very Well, if it is Translated Correctly by Experts, who might find it Difficult to Translate Hebrew into English: beCause, each Hebrew Word has 1, 2, 5, 10, 20, 50, or even more than 100 Different Definitions to Choose from, which is made even more Difficult by the Fact that the VOWELS were left OUT. Yes, here is that Phrase in English, wth th Vwls lft t. Can you now Understand WHY there is no Perfect Translation from Hebrew into English? Indeed, it was a very Confounded Language, you might say, which was Totally Inspired by SATAN, who is the Author of Confusion — not GOD, who is ALL that is GOOD, while the Devil is ALL that is EVIL! ‡§§

01-05 |_| For Example, you might Imagine that the above Photograph shows a GOOD House, which is Actually a BAD House: beCause it is not FIREPROOF, even though it is very Pretty; but, Pretty will not Save the Lives of the Poor Ignorant Children, who Die from Breathing the Toxic Smoke that comes from the Burning Carpets on the Floors, when such a Hateful House goes Up to Heaven in the Flames of Damnation, in Great Billowing Black Clouds of TOXIC SMOKE — even as tens of thousands of American Houses do, each Year; and yet the Ignorant FOOLS Vow to God to Rebuild those Houses, and get them Prepared for Tornadoes, Floods, Hurricanes, Earthquakes, and whatever might Happen to Destroy them by CHANCE and Lady LUCK, who has no Idea what a GOOD House is: beCause she never Visited the Shrine of Immaculate Conceptions in Washington, District of Chief Criminals, who LOVE those Hateful Taxes and all such Natural Disasters: beCause, they are Working for those Lying Conniving EDOMITES, whom God HATES, according to *Romans 9:13,* which is the Truth of it: beCause God HATES ALL THAT IS EVIL, and LOVES ALL THAT IS GOOD. Therefore, be Wise, as Saint Paul said, and *"Prove all Provable Things, while Clinging Tightly to ALL that is GOOD." — First Thessalonians 5:21,* which I have MAGNIFIED for you Ignorant FOOLS, who cannot Smell Out the Truth of it! †§‡§§

01-06 |_| O Moses, all of us Readers, who are Familiar with the Inspired Writings of the Man with the Spirit of Elijah, Understand that he is only Impersonating you: beCause, you are not Actually Writing anything: beCause, you were a Jewish Fabrication of those Lying Conniving Edomites, who Wanted to SELL BOOKS, who Invented their own Stories, which were mostly Handed Down from Traditional Pagan

MYTHS — such as that Noah's Ark Story, which came from Ancient Babylon, which is a Good Story for Teaching Lessons to Ignorant Children; but, it is not Based on Scientific Gilgamesh Realities: beCause, there is no Way on this Good Earth that an Old Man of 600 Years of Age, could Feed and Water 2 Million or more Animals in Cages, in some Imaginary Ark, which would have Required no less than 1,000,000 Gallons of Water per DAY, just to Water all of those Thirsty Animals. For Example, a single Cow can Drink 30 to 50 Gallons of Water per Day, and Piss Out an almost Equal Amount of Smelly TOXIC Urine, which someone would have to Mop Up; or else the Ark would be Filled with Methane Gases, which would KILL everything in the Ark, including the 40,000 Holy Angels, who might be Helping Poor Old Noah and his 3 Crazy Sons, who would be Driven Crazy by the Squawking Cackling Chickens, Gobbling Turkeys, Guinea Fowls, Peacocks, Ducks, Pheasants, Geese, Screech Owls, Hawks, Eagles, Buzzards, Crows, Ravens, and a half-million other Noisy Birds — not to Mention those Howler Monkeys, Apes, Trumpeting Elephants, Braying Asses, Elks, Mooses, and a thousand Kinds of Deers, Sheeps, Bleating Goats, and Snorting Smiling Camels! Yes, it would have been a First-Class Swanky NIGHTMARE, O Moses, and thou Knowest it: beCause, you are no Ignorant Fool! †§‡§§

01-07 [_] Well, my Friend, that is what I was Trying to Say, before I got Interrupted, which I really do not Object to: beCause, everyone should have a Right to Speak, which is called *Freedom of SPEECH,* which is Guaranteed in the CONSTITUTION for "The Divided States of United Lies!" (The so-called "United States of North America" in Disguise!) By The Worldwide People's Revolution!® Book 058, which is Designed to Keep the Masses of People Contented with a Modern Form of False Government, which I can Prove to be False in just one Sentence, if you will be so Patient as to Hear it, and Think about it: beCause, in spite of all of the Exaggerations and Sarcastic Humor within this Inspired Book, you can Discover Provable Truths that no Sane Person can Rightly Deny: beCause, it is Impossible to Defeat "The Swanky Sword of Divine Truths!" (The Most-Powerful Weapon in the Whole Universe!) By The Worldwide People's Revolution!® Book 067. Therefore, do not even Try it: beCause, that Sword of Truths will Cut Off your own Head of Lies, if you are not very Careful about the WAY that you Handle it. †§‡§§

01-08 [_] O Moses, if the Lying Conniving Edomites made up all of the Fictitious Stories about the Israelites being in Egypt, and Living in the Wilderness of Sin for 40 Years, on nothing but Manna, whom can we

Trust to Reveal the Whole Truth to us, and nothing but the Whole Truth?
‡

01-09 [_] Well, my Skeptical Friend, you can Trust GOD: beCause, he never Lies: beCause he hardly ever Speaks, and only Speaks a few Wise Words, whenever he does Speak: beCause he Wants People to THINK and Remember Things; but, most People have no Interest in Thinking. Nevertheless, all Provable Truths can be and should be Proven, at: "The GREAT Worldwide TELEVISED Court HEARING!" (That Great Meeting of the Most-Intelligent and Well-Educated Minds!) By The Worldwide People's Revolution!® Book 041B, which will be an Ongoing Thing within "The Great World TEMPLE of PEACE!" whose Elected Officials will take the Time to Address each and every Important Subject, including those Election Deceptions.

01-10 [_] O Moses, I want to Learn what is WRong with DUMBmocracy and Satanic Capitalism?

♦♦ — Chapter 02 — ♦♦

What is WRong with Election Deceptions!

02-01 |_| Well, let us say that you have a Dozen Ignorant Children: beCause of Quadruplets being Born, each Time, 3 Years in a Row, whereby you might have your Hands Full, as they say, just to Wash the Diapers and their little Soft Butts, who are Bound to Grow UP, and Discover that they can VOTE for how many Candies, Cokes, Cookies, Iced-creams, Pies, and Sweet Cakes that they might Want to Eat: beCause, they have Heard that all Men were Created Equal with Jesus Christ and Moses, who had no Idea what GOOD GOVERNMENT is all about, according to the Politicians in Washington, who simply Disregard *Numbers 16,* and *Leviticus 25:* beCause those Words do not Fit in with their Edomite Plan; but, that is what this Extremely Good Book is all about, whereby Innocent Humble and Honest Children might Agree with it: beCause, they Know for a Fact that they cannot Defeat "The Swanky Sword of Divine Truths!" which Proposes that if we are going to have Elections, the Most-Qualified People among us are the Innocent and HONEST CHILDREN, who have no Selfish Greedy Ambitions, nor Monetary Motives: beCause they are NOT Capitalists, until they are Tawt to be Greedy Selfish Capitalists. However, most Children are a little Selfish, who will even take the Candy away from another Child that is Younger and Weaker, if he Wants it: beCause, that is the Nature of most Children, who must be Tawt to SHARE their Toys and Things with the other Children, just to make them Civilized. Nevertheless, let us say that those Children were 12, 13 and 14 Years Old, and you gave to them a VOTE concerning how many Candies that they should Eat — would any of them Grow Up to become Adults with Teeths in their Heads? Probably not: beCause those Sugary Candies would most likely ROT OUT their Precious Teeths, and Especially if they were really Gooey STICKY Candies, which Taste so "GOOD" in the Mouth; but, are so Bitter in the Belly of the Mind, when the Teeth have ROTTED Out, and those Ignorant Children have to Rely on "Dentures," just to EAT! †§‡§§

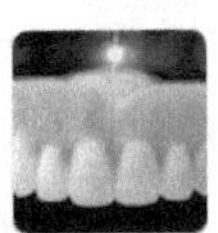

www.123dentist.com › everything-about-dentures ▾
Everything You Need To Know About Dentures ...
May 27, 2016 - **Dentures** are artificial teeth and gums that are formed to your mouth and created by your dentists to replace lost or removed natural teeth. **Dentures** can either be full or partial, meaning they can either replace all teeth on either the top or bottom gum line, or just a few that are missing.

02-02 |_| O Holy Moses, would you Expect the Children to Liv for 120 Years without getting any Candies to Eat, at all? What Kind of a Cruel Master are you? My Mother Fed me Candies when I was Young, and I still have all of my Teeth: beCause she also Tawt me to Brush my Teeth after Eating anything, which I have always Done for my Teeth's Sake, and will Continue to Do: beCause I Believe that a Child should Learn to Love and OBEY his Parents, even if he Thinks that they might be a little Crazy: beCause they are Older and have more Experience in Living, than Children.

02-03 |_| Well, my Friend, suppose that your Mother had not Tawt to you anything about Brushing your Precious Teeth; but, had just given to you a VOTE for whatever you might Want? How many Teeth do you Think that you might have, right now; and especially if the Candy Machine was for Free, and in the Kitchen, at Home, whereby you might get all of the Candies that you might Vote for, as well as anything else that you might Vote for? Suppose you went to Work for a Company that gave to you and all other Employees the RIGHT to VOTE for your Wages — how long would that Company Stay in Business? Moreover, suppose that they gave to you the Right to make Fake Tools, which just Fall Apart when you Use them: beCause of being Slopped Together like those Wooden / Plastic Houses, which should be against the law to build them? But, your not-so-Fatherly Federal Government is Working for the Insurance Companies, who LOVE those Fake Houses! §‡

02-04 [_] O Moses, are you saying that it might be Possible for us Education Slaves, Work Slaves, Tax Slaves, Insurance Slaves, Rent Slaves, Home-owner Slaves, Interest Slaves, Mortgage Slaves, ElecTrickery Bills Slaves, Food Bills Slaves, Water Bills Slaves, Gas Bills Slaves, Telephone Bills Slaves, Transportation Bills Slaves, Repair Bills Slaves, Entertainment Bills Slaves, Drug Bills Slaves, Doctor Bills Slaves, Hospital Bills Slaves, Childcare Bills Slaves, Nursing Home Bills Slaves, and Funeral Home Bills Slaves, to Build our own "Beautiful Swanky PALACES!" (A New Concept in Living Habits — Swanky Palaces for Poor People!) By The Worldwide People's Revolution!® Book 066, whereby we have NO BILLS, at all? After all, I am Happy to be one or all of those Kinds of SLAVES: beCause, I Liv in America, where I am Free to Pay all of my Endless BILLS, and Consume all of my Countless PILLS! Yes, my Favorite Song is that one that is Played at every Donald Trump Political Rally, which goes like this: ♫ *I'm so Proud to be an American, where at least I Know that I am Free!* So were the Children, who Burned up in American House Fires; or, just Died from the Toxic FUMES: beCause of God Blessing America! Yes, there are Millions of such House Fires, each Year — such as that Wonderful Disaster in Paradise, Californicate, in 2018, which Killed MILLIONS of Silly Children and Old Farts! †§‡§§

> It has been 355 days since the deadliest wildfire in **California's** history began. It ignited in the early morning hours of Nov. 8, 2018 and would rage for more than two weeks, devastating the town of **Paradise** before it was extinguished. Oct 29, 2019

> www.pbs.org › wgbh › frontline › article › camp-fire-b... ▾
> Camp Fire: By the Numbers | Fire in Paradise ...

02-05 [_] Well, my Friend, you might find it Funny; but, those thousands of Proud Home-owners were not so Happy with it, who would Prefer to be Living in those "Beautiful Swanky Stone Dome Home COMPLEXES!" (HOW to Build SECURE Tax-proof, Insurance-proof, Self-air-conditioned, Paint-proof, Rot-proof, Termite-proof, Mouse-proof, Fireproof, Tornado-proof, Hurricane-proof, Thief-proof, and BOMB-PROOF Houses!) By The Worldwide People's Revolution!® Book 102 — except that they never Heard of them: beCause, the Snooze Reporters Failed to Mention them, and not even John McArdle on the *Washington Journal* Mentioned them, in spite of Knowing about them: beCause, he is just another Spiritual COWARD!

02-06 [_] That Picture shows a small Part of the 2,000-square-feet Rock and Concrete Roof that our Selected King Built at *330 Famous Rock House Road,* near Central, Arkansas, which is about 7 Miles from Horatio, Arkansas, which Suffered a Bad Hailstorm, which Beat on the Roofs of their Houses, which Caused them to Waste a Million Dollars or more to Fix them; and then, Believe it or not, an Ice Storm Struck, which Caved-in Roofs, Fell Trees, and Ruined practically every House in that City of Idiots, who still did not Wake Up nor come to their Right Senses with the Prodigal Son of *Luke 15,* which is easier to Understand in: "The New MAGNIFIED Version of The GOOD NEWS According to Saint LUKE!" (The Magnified Gospel of Saint Luke in Plain English!) By The Worldwide People's Revolution!® Book 061; but, how many Work Slaves and Tax Slaves have TIME to Study it? Have YOU Studied it, O Man of Greater Faith? §§

02-07 |_| O Moses, not everyone can Afford to Build nor Buy a Million-dollar 98% Rock House, like that of your Selected King. For Example, there is his 40,000$ Ceramic Shower Room! And the following Picture shows a Part of one of his 7 Spanish Marble Walls, which Costed 1,500$ for just ONE Tile, which is 18-inches square, and he has HUNDREDS of them! And after that, you can see a Picture of his Italian Marble Living Room Floor, which Costed 100,000 Dollars! Therefore, if you are going to Talk to us about True Prosperity, O Moses, you will have to Address the MONEY Issue: beCause, none of us Credit Card Debt Slaves have any Idea WHERE to get so much MONEY, and especially if we Liv in Poor Countries in Africa and Asia — such as India and Bangladesh, who do well to Feed ourselves! However, I will Confess that we do have hundreds of thousands of Mountains of Rocks to Work with, if only we could figure out HOW to Harvest them, which would Require the Assistance of those **"Seven Great Armies of Working Soldiers!" (HOW to Provide a Way for Everyone to WORK: so as to Eliminate Poverty, Crimes, Drug Abuses, Prisons and Unnecessary Taxes!) By The Worldwide People's Revolution!® Book 015B, which is a Companion Book of: "The Swanky Associations of Working Soldiers!" (A Fascinating Collection of Various Kinds of Voluntary Working Soldiers!) By The Worldwide People's Revolution!® Book 018B,** which no Church of God nor Bar Room can Afford! †§‡§§

{The Real Beauty of the Spanish Marble cannot be Seen, until you take
a Microscopic View of it with Telescopic Eyeballs, after Fasting for 40
Days or so, just to get your Eyeballs Working Correctly, like mine.
Moreover, that is no Joke, which you will not Fully Realize, until you
Do it, yourself: beCause, I cannot Do it for you, nor can anyone else.
Trust me, it is some of the Most-Beautiful Marble in the whole World!}

{The Italians have a Great Appreciation for Beautiful Marbles. The
Walls were not faced with Spanish Marble when this Photo was taken.
Not very many American Families have a Living Room that is 588
square feet; but, they could have, if they just Obeyed me. The Kitchen
is 168 sq. ft., which is half as big as the Average House in Africa!}

23

02-08 [_] There is a Part of our Selected King's Unfinished Marble Office, which looks a lot better in Person, and up close: beCause the Beauty of the Marble cannot be Seen very Well at a Distance.

02-09 [_] Just Imagine how Bad-looking that Million-dollar Onyx Box would be from 100 feet away from it. Here is a Portion of our Selected King's Algerian Onyx Bedroom Floor in all of its Naked Glory, before it got Stolen from him by those Lying Conniving Legalized Edomites. †§‡§§

02-10 [_] You cannot See the Great Beauty in a Picture; but, the Beauty is there up Close to Study.

♦♦♦ — Chapter 03 — ♦♦♦

Did you get to Vote for Living in such a Good House?

03-01 [_] NO — you never Heard about any such Houses: beCause the Teachers and Government Officials just Assumed that it is Impractical to Build such Houses, even though it is not: beCause, there are hundreds of thousands of Mountains of Rocks to Work with, if we have the Faith to Do it. Here is a Photo of a Part of the 70 feet of Countertops, which is Indian Marble at its Best. †§‡

03-02 [_] O Moses, if I Wanted to Liv in such a House, the first thing that I would do, is to go to my Friendly Banker, and Borrow enough Money for making myself into an Education Slave, whereby I might get myself one of those Edomite Diplomas, whereby I might get myself a Good Job with Uncle Jobe, whereby I might make myself into a Work Slave, Rent Slave, ElecTrickery Bills Slave, Food Bills Slave, Water Bills Slave, Gas Bills Slave, Transportation Bills Slave, Repair Bills Slave, Telephone Bills Slave, and all of those other Kinds of Slaves that are only Mentioned in Verse 02-04, who are the Healthiest and Happiest People in the Whole World: beCause of Eating with the Dogs and Hogs at the Death and Hell Restaurants, who never Tasted of a Really GOOD Fruit during their entire Liivz: beCause of not Electing a Righteous King to Govern them. Indeed, they should get Smart, and "VOTE for The GOAT!" (The New Political Party that has Guaranteed Solutions for our Massive Problems!) By The Worldwide People's Revolution!® Book 109, who would Ask for "Seven Great Armies of Working Soldiers!" who would Voluntarily Help to Build those "GLORIOUS Swanky Hotels Castles and Fortresses!" (Beautiful Planned City States for WISE Intelligent Well-Educated People with Common Sense and Good Understanding!) By The Worldwide People's Revolution!® Book 019B: beCause they are "The Right Design for Living!" (A List of Great Advantages for Building Beautiful Planned City States!) By The Worldwide People's Revolution!® Book 012B, which have more than 5,000 Advantages over these Hateful Cities of Confusion, which do not have any Luscious All-Mineral Organic Gardens within them: beCause they are Designed by Satan and Sons, Incorporated, who also never got to Eat any Mangos at those "Royal Swanky Buffets!" (The Best Feasts in the Whole World!) By The Worldwide People's Revolution!® Book 103.

03-03 [_] So, did they even get to VOTE for Eating any such Mangos? Were they on the Election Deception Ballot? NO, of course not: beCause it is only Good for Electing Politicians and Ignorant Fools, who never got to Study: "All of the Arguments are in Favor of our Selected King, who has Zero Challengers!" (Before you Attend another Election Deception, you should Carefully Study this Inspired Book with an Honest Open Mind!) By The Worldwide People's Revolution!® Book 085: beCause it was never Advertised on TV, nor was: "How all Women can Get True Justice without Getting Divorced from God!" (The Unjust Case of Judge Brett Kavanaugh and Doctor Christine Blasey Ford is now Revisited by a Wise Son of King Solomon!) By The Worldwide People's Revolution!® Book 087. In Fact, not even the Irreverent Snake ever once Mentioned: "A New Jerusalem in the Great State of Flexible Texas!" Book 090: beCause, he does not Believe in it, much less, in: "The Great World TEMPLE of PEACE!" which he Mocks as a Thing of Nothing Important, in spite of the Fact that Jesus Christ will not Return, until his Bride has made herself HOLY, even as he is Holy: beCause he is not going to Govern a Horde of Ignorant FOOLS, who are still Eating with the Dogs and Hogs, when he Clearly said: *"Come you Out from among the Wicked Ones, and be you Separated from them, says the Supreme Ruler, and Touch NONE of their Unclean Things; and then I will Receive you, and will be a Loving Father unto you, and you shall become my Adopted Sons and Holy Dawterz, says the Supreme Judge of this Heaven and Earth."* — NMV of Second Corinthians 6:17—7:1, which reads: *"Therefore, having those Promises, Dearly Beloved Brothers — that God will Accept us as his*

own Adopted Sons and Purified Dawterz, and also Walk with us — let us Cleanse ourselves from ALL Filthiness of the Flesh and Spirit, while Perfecting Holiness in the Fear of God, which begins with Purity of Mind, Body and Spirit, which is Obtained by Fasting and Praying, until we are Baptized with Fire, which only God can Do, who will also Fill us with his Holy Spirit, when we Overcome all of our Sins — even, in as much as we Overcome all of our Sins: beCause, it is another Case of INASMUCH AS, which Means to whatever Degree that we Cleanse ourselves." ‡

{He is 154 Years Old this Month, with Perfect Vision! †§‡}

03-04 [_] O Moses, when you came Down from Mount Sinai, your Face was Shining with the Glory of God, whereby the Children of Israel could not Tolerate the Pain of Looking at you: beCause it Hurt their Eyeballs. Therefore, they put a Veil over your Face: so that they could not See your Face, which Reflected the Glory of God, which they could not Tolerate, which Happened to you after Fasting for 40 Consecutive Days and Nights, twice in a Row, according to *Deuteronomy 9:9 and 18;* but, it did not Happen to the People of Nineveh, who also Fasted without Eating nor Drinking for 40 Days, according to *the Book of Jonah,* which Killed a lot of Aborted Babies, which Jesus did not Speak Evil of: beCause it was a Good Thing: beCause those Holy Mothers got Pregnant again with Holy Babies, who were Born without any Physical nor Mental Defects: beCause they were Conceived by HOLY Seeds from Holy Fathers, which Pleased Jehovah God very much: beCause that is the Whole Purpose for us Living in this World — to become HOLY, even as God is HOLY, which anyone can Prove According to the *Scriptures.* †§‡

03-05 [_] You have got to be Kidding us! Indeed, the Purpose for us to be Born into this World is to Produce Beautiful Churches to Attend, and Holy Mosques, Shrines, Temples, Cathedrals and Tabernacles, which is Proven by *Acts 7:48 and 17:24,* which is the Conclusion of that Subject. †§‡§§

03-06 [_] O Holy Moses, you are being very Sarcastic again. Can you not Resist the Temptation to Mock our Ignorance? Indeed, if God does not Dwell in Temples that are made with Hands, it must be that he Livz within us; but, only IF we are Holy, even as he is Holy. See *First Peter 1:15—16,* which is speaking only about our Conversations, and not our Deeds: beCause, there is no Connection between our Works and our Words, even as there is no Connection between the Beliefs of the People who Built that Beautiful Ceramic Church, which is even more Beautiful on the Inside, than on the Outside: beCause, it is like Jupiter, which gets more and more Beautiful as one gets into the hundred or more Concentric Worlds within Worlds — all of which are Guarded by Holy Angels with Flaming Swords: beCause, no Unclean Things can Enter into those Worlds, which are Prepared for Holy People, who have Overcome all of their Sins, and have Stopped Sinning, which is a Good Thing; but, it is not Tawt in very many Churches: beCause they do not Believe in HOLINESS of Mind, Spirit, nor BODY. In Fact, they Believe that we are not Defiled by whatever we Eat; but, only by what we Think and Speak, which Jesus Christ Confirmed. †§‡§§

{He is 48 Years Old, and must Wear Triple-Bifocal-Glasses, just to Read the Headline News, in Big Print, which has never once Mentioned Arnold Ehret, much less: **"The Proper RULES for FASTING!"** Book 046. After all, they only Publish "Truths," with no Lies! †§‡§§}

03-07 |_| For Example, there is a Photo of a True Christian, who was going Shopping for more to EAT: beCause of being HUNGRY, and nearly Starving to Death for a Lack of Enzymes, Vitamins, and Minerals, which could not Reach his Brains: beCause of being Obstructed by Buckets of Accumulated Slime and Stinking FILTH, whereby he Appears to be Pregnant with no less than 12 Children, who has not Seen his Tally Whacker nor Chime Bells in more than 20 Years, which are Hidden under all of that Obnoxious FAT: beCause, he is Related with a WALRUS! However, you could never Persuade him that Jesus was Correct, when he said: *"It is not that which Enters into your Mouth that is Causing you to Defile yourself; but, it is the Evil Thots that come Out of an Evil Mind, which gives to you an Evil Appetite."* — *The Gospel According to Saint Bartholomew.* §§‡

03-08 |_| Well, my Friend, he is a very Deceived Person, and in several Different Ways; but, you could never Persuade him of it: beCause, he is quite Certain that he is Saved and going to Heaven when he Dies: beCause, he has never Studied an Inspired Book, called: "Do People Go to Heaven when they Die?" (The Unbelievable Truth about Life and Death!) **By The Good Pastor of Uncommon Sense!** Book 120. Indeed, here is an Artist's Conception of "Heaven." |_| Amen. †§‡

Giovanni Battista Tiepolo, summoned specially from Venice for the purpose, decorated the vault in 1752/53 with the **largest** ceiling **fresco ever** painted. With great artistic sensitivity he depicted the exotic, magical **worlds** of the continents of America, Asia and Africa, personified by regal female figures.

www.residenz-wuerzburg.de › residenz › treppe ▾
Bavarian Palace Administration | Würzburg Residence ...

03-09 [_] It is the Largest Fresco in the World, and was Painted during just one Day! But, you do not have to Believe that: beCause, you can Check Out the Facts on the Internet for yourself. †§‡§§

03-10 [_] O Moses, if I had to get into the Internet, just to Check Out the FACTS for everything that I Hear or See on the TV, I would never get anything Done. Therefore, it all Calls for: "The GREAT Worldwide TELEVISED Court HEARING!" (That Great Meeting of the Most-Intelligent and Well-Educated Minds!) By The Worldwide People's Revolution!® Book 041B

{**FOOTNOTE 02.** Those are Real Marble Pillars, and Real Gold, in a Wurzburg Church, in Germany, which is not far from the Marienberg Fortress, which was never Conquered during 400 Years: beCause, it was Protected by Holy Angels, who have their Statues in the above Church, along with their Holy Bishops, which you can Prove in a Courtroom, if you Want to. Otherwise, you can just Accept my Words for it, and go ahead and be Deceived, just like most People. §§}

Marienberg **Fortress** (German: Festung Marienberg) is a prominent landmark on the left bank of the Main river in **Würzburg**, in the Franconia region of Bavaria, Germany. The mighty **Fortress** Marienberg is a symbol of **Würzburg** and served as a home of the local prince-bishops for nearly five centuries.

en.wikipedia.org › wiki › Marienberg_Fortress ▾
Marienberg Fortress - Wikipedia

♦♦♦♦ — Chapter 04 — ♦♦♦♦

Is there such a Thing as Homeland Security?

04-01 [_] Believe it or not, the Residence Building for the Bishops Survived World War 2, when most of Wurzburg was Totally Destroyed by American Angels, who Dropped some 50,000 Tons of Bombs on the College Town, in the Holy Names of Freedom, Liberty, and Justice for ALL! †§‡

Würzburg is also the capital of the German wine region Franconia which is **famous for** its mineralic dry white wines especially from the Silvaner grape. Würzburger Hofbräu brewery also locally produces a **well-known** pilsner beer. **Würzburg** is home of the oldest Pizzeria in Germany.

en.wikipedia.org › wiki › Würzburg
Würzburg - Wikipedia

04-02 [_] So, O Holy Moses, if Americans could Cold-heartedly Bomb some Peaceful Old City like Wurzburg, which covers about 87 square Kilometers, just Think about what Saintly Things that they could Do in Florence, Italy, and in Rome, whereby they could REJOICE over the Destruction of Saint Peter's Basilica: beCause of having no Respect for the Hard Labors of other People, who had nothing to Do with those Wicked Nazis, whom God Ordained to Destroy his Chosen People, called the JEWS, according to *Romans 13,* which makes it quite Clear that God Ordains the Leaders of all Nations, including Saint Joseph Stalin, who had some 50 Million White Russian Christians put to DEATH in the Holy Names of Freedom, Liberty and Justice for ALL: beCause, those Russian Communists Sang the very same Song that Americans Sang, which is WHY that the American Government took the Side of Saint Stalin during World War 2, in spite of all of the Warning Signs about his Evilness, who Starved to Death Millions of Ukrainians for the Sake of Communism, which has been Proven in YouTube Videos, if you Care to Learn about that Cigar-chomping, Vodka-drinking, Cursing Foul-mouthed Stalin, who was a Close Friend of that other Cigar-chomping, Whiskey-guzzling, Cursing Churchill, whom Americans also Supported during World War 2: beCause, those 2 Characters were "the Lesser of the 5 Evils," according to President Franklin Edomite Roosevelt, who Knew for a Fact that Adolf Hitler was Ordained by God: beCause, all that he was Asking for was a *Worldwide*

Radio Debate between himself and the Leaders of France, Great Britain, Russia, and "The Divided States of United Lies!" (The so-called "United States of North America" in Disguise!) By The Worldwide People's Revolution!® Book 058, who all Knew full Well that the *Versailles Peace Treaty,* which was Signed after World War 1, had everything Set Up Perfectly for World War 2: beCause, the Treaty DEMANDED the Defeated Germans to Pay REPARATIONS for Damages during World War 1, at the Rate of more than their Total National Income! For Example, suppose that the United States had Lost World War 2, and those Nazis made up a *Nuremburg Peace Treaty,* which Required Americans to Pay Reparations for the Damages that they did during World War 2, which Amounted to more than all of the Income Taxes that have been Collected since World War 2? Yes, how would you Americans Like that Peace Treaty? Awe, you would Naturally be Fired Up for World War 3: beCause of making the Grave Mistake of Bombing Wurzburg, Germany, which alone would Cost you no less than 20 Trillion Dollars: beCause of Ruining Ancient Landmarks in Germany, which could not be Replaced, even as the Capitol Building in Washington could not be Replaced, if a Hydrogen Bomb were to BLAST IT OFF OF THE EARTH! Indeed, a Similar Capitol Building might be Rebuilt; but, the Original Capitol would be GONE, forever! Likewise, if Saint Peter's Basilica in Rome were to be Bombed Off of the Earth, WHO could Replace it? Who could Afford the Costs of REPARATIONS? Therefore, you should all Study: "HOW to Make Proper REPARATIONS!" (True Justice for Black and White People, and Everyone in Between them!) By The Worldwide People's Revolution!® Book 122, and: "What would Moses and Jesus Do with the Statues and Monuments???" (A Unique Plan for Solving the Problem, which Everyone can be Extra Happy with!) By Liberty and Justice is for ALL! Book 123, which are both Amazing Books, which will Hold Up in any Courtroom with a Righteous Juj in Charge of it. In Fact, for not Agreeing to Face Adolf Hitler in a Worldwide Radio Debate, Fair and Square, American Tax Slaves will have to Pay Germans Total Reparations for all of the Damages that they Caused during World War 2; or else I, Moses, will take the Side of Germany, and God will WIPE YOU PEOPLE OUT with "The Great ATOMIC NIGHTMARE!" (The Saddest Story in World History!) By The Great White Bald Eagle! Book 099: beCause of not Quickly Agreeing that it was WRong for the Leaders of France, Great Britain, Russia, and the United States to Deny Adolf Hitler of that Peaceful Meeting of the Most-Intelligent Minds, whereby 60 Million Lives could have been Saved from World War 2! Yes, I, MOSES, will take the Right Side of History, and God Almighty will be on my Side, along with whomever else takes the Right Side of History, and Does what is RIIT for all of the People! Otherwise, God would not be a God of True Justice, would he? But, he is a God of True Justice, who will get Revenge in his own Way, which may be something much Worse than Bug-19. (See YouTube for "History of the Black Death," and do not Think that God cannot Arrange another Great Plague: beCause he is Really GOOD at Things like that! Yes, you can Accept my Words for it: beCause, I am the Man who took the Children of Israel through the Bottom of the Red Sea, at Easy-on Geber, if'n ye Recall; but, if you do not Recall it, why not take the Time to Study: "The New MAGNIFIED Version of GENESIS!" (The Enlightening Version of the Beginnings of Things!) By The Worldwide People's Revolution!® Book 088, whereby you might Learn something Good? †§‡§§

04-03 |_| O Moses, there is no such a Thing as Homeland Security, if God is Against us, even if we go to Work, and Build those "GLORIOUS Swanky Hotels Castles and Fortresses!": beCause Mosquitoes can Transport Strange Viirusez into the Fortresses, by Means of Hateful Birds that Fly them into those Fortresses. Therefore, the only Sure Homeland Security is to take the Riit Siid uv HISTREE, and Do what is Right for ALL of the Peoples, Worldwide, who all Need their own Secure Swanky Fortresses with Large Swanky Cisterns in Great Stone Terraces, whereby they have at least a 7-Year Supply of Fresh Living WATER: beCause, just after AIR, Water is the single most Important Thing, which can be Kept Fresh and Alive by Pumping it from Lower Swanky Cisterns, UP to Higher Swanky Cisterns, whereby it can Run over Pleasant Waterfalls, and through Rocky Creeks with Sand and Gravel to Purify the Water, just as it is now Done by Nature in the Wilderness of Jasper National Park in Canada, which has a few of the Last Glaciers on this Good Earth: beCause People have Failed to Study, "How Best to Prepare for CLIMATE CHANGES!" (The Wisest Plan for Mankind to Follow!) By The Worldwide People's Revolution!® Book 004B, which is a Companion Book of: "UNLIMITED ENERGY 99 Percent Pollution-Free!" (HOW to Obtain Free ElecTrickery, Worldwide!) By The Worldwide People's Revolution!® Book 029B, which should be the Number 1 Best Seller. †§§‡

04-04 |_| Well, my Friend, maybe they should First Study: "The Washington Journal is a FARCE! (C-SPAN Managers are not very WISE!) By The Worldwide People's Revolution!® Book 006C, which is a Companion Book of: "Why do I have to be Surrounded by CRAZY PEOPLE!" (Do almost all People Feel like they are Surrounded by CRAZY People?) By The Worldwide People's Revolution!® Book 005B, which is a Companion Book of : "For the Love of Money!" (The Strange Things that People Say and Do to Get more Money!) By The Worldwide People's Revolution!® Book 003B, which is a Companion Book of: "The Root Cause for almost all Evils!" Book 078, which is a Companion Book of: "Guaranteed Solutions!" (HOW to Solve our Local and Global Problems in the Most-Rational Manner Possible!) By The Worldwide People's Revolution!® Book 080, which is a Companion Book of: "The GREAT Worldwide TELEVISED Court HEARING!" which is at the Heart of Solving every Problem there is: beCause it makes it Possible for us Slaves to Learn the Truth! †§‡

04-05 |_| O Moses, just as Adolf Hitler was Denied that Great Radio Debate, your Selected King will no doubt also be Denied **"The GWTCH!"** beCause those Lying Conniving Edomites will not Want to Learn any Provable Truths about anything: beCause, it is just like Jesus said — that Evil People do not Want to come into the Light of Truths, lest their Evil Deeds should be Exposed. †§‡

04-06 [_] Well, my Friend, the Logistics are much Different, right now: beCause most People have Telephones with Social Media — such as Facebook — whereby they can easily Communicate for Free, and Spread Messages far and wide within Days, or even within Minutes. Therefore, it is more likely that we can get Leaders to Cooperate with "The GREAT Worldwide TELEVISED Court HEARING!" which will Solve a LOT of Problems: beCause of Exposing the Lies of those Edomites — such as the Need for Bankers, when no Bankers are Needed for True Prosperity; but, LOTS of Money is Desperately Needed, and Provided by "The New RIGHTEOUS One-World Government!" which does what is RIIT for ALL of the Peoples, Worldwide. Guaranteed! †§‡§§

04-07 [_] O Moses, without Bankers to Loan Money, almost none of those Big Bank Buildings would have ever been Built, and not even those thousands of Apartment Houses would have been Built: beCause, very few People have Saved enough Money for Building any such Big Buildings.

04-08 [_] Well, my Friend, what you are saying is 100% True. However, it is the Constitutional Duty of "The New RIGHTEOUS One-World Government!" to Mint and Print the Necessary New Money for Hiring "Seven Great Armies of Working Soldiers!" (HOW to Provide a Way for Everyone to WORK: so as to Eliminate Poverty, Crimes, Drug Abuses, Prisons and Unnecessary Taxes!) By The Worldwide People's Revolution!® Book 015B, to Build those "Beautiful Swanky

Stone Dome Home COMPLEXES!" all around the World, within those "**GLORIOUS Swanky Hotels Castles and Fortresses!**" whereby everyone can have True Security, and not Liv in Fear of Raccoons Eating their Corn, nor Poisonous Snakes getting into their Luscious All-Mineral Organic Gardens, which are Protected by the Tall Stone Walls with Moats around them: beCause, the only Way to get into or out of any of those Beautiful Planned City States, is through Long Underground Tunnels, which go to the Central Hotels for Visitors, which Long Tunnels have Traps within them for Catching any Rats, Snakes, and whatever might get into them: beCause those Tunnels are Inspected with Hidden Security Cameras and Wide-Awake Security Guards, who can be Trusted to Do their Duties: beCause each of "**The Swanky Associations of Working Soldiers!**" (**A Fascinating Collection of Various Kinds of Voluntary Working Soldiers!**) **By The Worldwide People's Revolution!®** Book 018B, have their Duties.

04-09 [_] O Moses, it Sounds to me like you and your Selected King have Plans for Establishing a Police State for everyone to Liv in, whereby the Masses of People have no Freedom to come and go, whereby they might Buy and Sell Drugs, Weapons, Booze, and whatever they Want to Sell.§‡

04-10 [_] And why in the World would a Healthy Young Man like him be Needing or Wanting any Freedom to Buy and/or Sell any Drugs, Weapons, Alcoholic Drinks, Sex, or whatever, when it is Possible for him to Grow his own Marijuana, at Home, if he Wants to get Drunk on it? Indeed, he could Feed it to his own Children, whereby their Brains might also not Develop Correctly, whereby they might also become Typical American Idiots and Drug Addicts, who have no Idea WHY that they were even Born into this World of Wonders; but, I will Explain it to you in the next Chapter, whereby you will Understand that you are Limiting the Blessings of God, while making Fools of yourselves, and for no Good Reasons — except for your Childish Stupidity! †§‡

◆◆◆◆◆ — Chapter 05 — ◆◆◆◆◆

WHY we were Born!

05-01 [_] First of all, in Order to Understand WHY we were Born, we must View the World from God's Perspective: beCause, he is the Great Creator and Divine Lawmaker, who is much more likely to Know what is going on, even as a Chair or Table is less likely to Know what is going on, than the Carpenter who Made the Chair or Table. Therefore, please give to me your Full Attention: beCause, I will Teach to you what God has to Say about it, who Revealed it to me, whereby you will come to Understand WHY we were Born, and what our Destinies are, Depending on what we Do with that Information: beCause, we are all Free to Choose whatever we Want to Believe, if we are not Blindfolded by those Edomite LIES, who are Slave Masters, who only Seek to make more and more Slaves, and not Humble Honest Men of True Wisdom, who Seek ALL that is GOOD! ‡

05-02 [_] O Moses, if I Actually Knew for a FACT that Almighty God Revealed something to you, I might Listen to you; but, I do not Believe that God Revealed anything to you: beCause, I am an Unbeliever, as you would Say, who Deserves to go to Hell with Satan, even as my own Father, who used God's Name in Vain, and Disregarded his Sabbath Days and Holy Days, and Basically made a Fool of himself, who Died with Cancers and Various Kinds of Ailments. †§‡§§

05-03 [_] Well, my Potential Friend, I Fully Understand what you are Saying: beCause, I also Question the "Authority" of People who Speak in the Name of God, who Profess to Believe in Jesus Christ, and even Confess that he is their Anointed Savior; but, their WORKS Betray their False Faith, whereby everyone, who takes a Good Honest Look at them, Knows for a Fact that they Missed the Central Message that Jesus was Teaching, which was about HOLINESS of Mind, Spirit and BODY, which Arnold Ehret Discovered after much Fasting and Praying, which set him Apart from the Normal Dietary Sinner, who does not Float on his Feet, like Arnold did, who had no Weight on his Feet, even though he could Feel that he was Touching the Floor: beCause his Senses were still Working, and Working a lot Better than the Senses of any Greasy Pork-Eater, who is often very Moody and Unstable, who cannot be Trusted to Tell the Whole Truth: beCause, he is Self-Deceived, who might even See White as being Black, or Black as being White: beCause of being like those Ancient Pharisees, who were Blinded by their PRIDE and IGNORANCE, who even Orchestrated the Crucifixion of the Most-Righteous Man who ever Lived! Therefore, there was something Drastically WRong with them, which they could not Understand, Analyze, nor Overcome: beCause of being all PUFFED UP with Great PRIDE, which Blinded their Minds. †§‡

05-04 [_] The Truth only Asks for a Fair HEARING. Therefore, Listen Carefully to me, whereby you might Hear the Whole Truth, which has the Power to Liberate you from your Prison of Lies. For Example, do you have any Idea what is Behind that Beautiful Marble Wall? Well, from Looking at the Photo that Follows Verse 02-06, you might GUESS what is on the other Side of that Marble Wall; but, you do not Know for a FACT what is over there, do you? Yes, there is a Toilet over there, and there might even be a Bidet and Sink for Washing; but, until you Actually SEE it, you do not Know for Sure, do you? Moreover, you could Assume that it is a Green Toilet and Sink: beCause there are Matching Colors of Green on the Walls; but, you would be Presumptuous to Assume that you Know for Sure what is over there, [ ] Riit; or, [ ] Rong? Go ahead and Check the Box that you Agree with, and be Perfectly Honest about it: beCause, unless you have Actually Seen what is over there, you cannot Honestly Say that you Know for Sure what is over there: beCause that is the Reality of it, which is the same for what Words follow here. †§‡

05-05 [ ] So, O Moses, are you saying that we have all been Presumptuous about WHY we were Born, who have no Real Idea WHY: beCause, God has not taken the Time to Show it to us? †§‡§§

05-06 [ ] Well, my Friend, God Revealed it to our Selected King, many Years Ago, which was contained in an Inspired Book, which was Posted on the Internet, in a Special Website, called: **www.ThePeacock.com**, which was taken Down: beCause the Capitalist, who was Sustaining it, was Riding the Fake Economic System, which you call "the Economic Salvation of Mankind," which has just recently Produced MILLIONS of Broke Capitalists, who have gone Out of Business for a Lack of MONEY: beCause the Capitalist System is Based on *"... the Love of Money,"* which is the Root Cause for almost all Evils: beCause, Poor People will Say and Do almost anything to Gain more Money and Wealth: beCause, like Socialists and Communists, they are Possession Worshipers, who have more Love for their Possessions, than they have for GOD: beCause, that is "The Nature of CAPITALISM!" (A List of the EVILS of CAPITALISM!) By The Worldwide People's Revolution!® Book 038, which is Unable to Save itself from the Bug-19, the Great Recession, the Great Depression, the Boom and Bust False Economy, or even from the Countless Divorces that come about for a LACK of MONEY: beCause, what can a Person DO without LOTS of MONEY? For Example, HOW would you go about Building that Large Cistern for Water Storage for your All-Mineral Organic Garden, if you had no Money for Building those 164 Hardened Concrete and Rock BLOCKS? Our Selected King did most of the Work, and Handled ALL of the Rocks in those Blocks, which Amounted to about 160 Tons, which Required 7 Years of HARD Work, just to Build it, which the Normal American would have no Interest in Building, unless he had LOTS of Money, whereby he might HIRE some Work Slaves to Build it.

05-07 |_| ♦♦♦♦♦♦♦ O Moses, I will now take the Time to Explain to you WHY we were Born. Therefore, Dig the Wax of Unbelief OUT of your Spiritual Ears, and Listen to me: beCause, no Person on this Good Earth can Prove my Words to be WRong: beCause they are Inspired by the Holy Spirit. In the Beginning, before there were any Worlds to be Inhabited, the Most-High God was Thinking about what he should Do to Create a Beautiful Universe, and HOW it should be Managed: beCause he was not the God of Stupidity, nor of Personal Lusts; but, he was the Great Master Farmer, himself, who said: *"Let there be Light,"* since there was nothing but GASES in the Vastness of Space, from which God Created the Galaxies, Nebulas, Stars, Planets, Earths, Moons, Comets, Asteroids, and all Visible Things: beCause everything must be BORN from something else: beCause, nothing has the Power to Create itself; and each Living Thing must have a SPIRIT, which Gives to it LIFE, which makes it a SOUL. Therefore, you are a Living Soul, and so is your Dog or Cat: beCause, without a Spirit, they would not be ALIVE. Moreover, that is the Part of all Living Things that Scientists cannot Make: beCause, they are not among the GODS, who Created their own Worlds, according to their own Desires: beCause the Most-High God Gave to them the Power to Do that: beCause he Wanted a Multitude of Worlds of Various Kinds, whereby he might Experiment with them, while Hoping that those Gods would Help him to Discover the Best Kind to Reproduce, Abundantly, in some Far-away Universe, which would be Far-beyond the Reach of Satan, who is also a Great Spirit Being, who

Believes that all Souls should be FORCED to Obey certain Laws and Rules, whereby they would have no Choices, even as a Cow must Obey Natural Dietary Laws, and cannot take up Eating at any "Royal Swanky Buffets!" (The Best Feasts in the Whole World!) By The Worldwide People's Revolution!® Book 103: beCause, she has no Hands for Earning Money, Buying Land, Fruit Trees, Nut Trees, Vegetable Seeds, Flowers, nor making any Tools to Work with; but, People can Do all of those Things with the Materials, Plants, Animals, and whatever God has Provided for us to Work with: beCause, we were Created to Manage the Worlds that we are Born into, each of which Requires a GOD to GOVERN it, who Willingly Chooses to Love and Obey the Laws of the Most-High God, without being FORCED to Do it: beCause, the Most-High God only Wants the Best of Good Men to be the Supreme Rulers of their own Worlds, which is WHY that he Chose Jesus Christ to be the Supreme Ruler of this World of Wonders: beCause, he has a Humble Honest Submissive Spirit, who says, *"... not my Will be Done; but, your Will be Done, O Master Farmer,"* which is a very Good Attitude: beCause, if everyone in the Whole World had such a Good Spirit, how many Poor People would there be? How many Hateful Wars would there be? How many Men would be Chomping on Stinking Cigars, and getting Drunk on Whiskey and Beers? How many Men would be Beating on their Disobedient Wives and Rebellious Children? How many Crimes would be Committed by Ignorant Fools? Who would be Collecting Taxes for Hiring Policemen to Watch over them? What would be Discussed on the C-SPAN TV and Radio Networks? What Need would there be for any Politicians, at all, since everyone would be Living in their own Private Paradises, within Beautiful Planned City STATES, each of which Governs itself, according to its own Elected Laws and Flexible Rules: beCause of being FREE to Choose whatever they Want, along with other People of Like-mindedness, who are Welcome to Discover and Choose whatever Religious and Political Beliefs that they Like; but, only with other People of Like-mindedness, whereby the People, who are Like Sheeps and Goats, are not Governed by Greedy Hogs nor Barking Dogs: beCause, they have Contrary Natures, which do not get along Well when they are Together, being much like God and Satan, who have always been at Odds with one another, who cannot Agree just HOW People should be Governed, who are much more Divided than the Dimwitcrats and Reprobates in Washington, District of Chief Criminals, who Vainly Imagine that all Men were Created EQUAL, when they were NOT. In Fact, each one is Special and Unique, who should be Free to Choose whatever they Want, even if they Want to have Gay Orgies, just to Prove what Fools that they are, who Like the Flavor of Sperm, and Enjoy Eating it, and also Enjoy Licking on each other's Anuses: beCause that is the Result of LUSTS, which are Longing Desires for Forbidden Things, whereby Dung Tastes Good to them, which is their own Business: beCause, God is just Winking at them: beCause, he Knows for a Fact that none of them will Enter into his HOLY Kingdom: beCause they are FILTHY People, who Liv for Sensual Pleasures, which cannot Satisfy the Soul, which can only be Satisfied with ALL that is GOOD, which is GOD, who Loves ALL that is Good, while Satan Loves ALL that is EVIL, including Lies and Deceptions, who Refuses to be Perfectly Honest about anything, who Vainly Imagines that it is a Good Thing for only a few Rich Hogs to have 90% of the Economic Pie, as an Economist might say, while 90% of the Masses of People are Living in EXTREME Poverty, who have never even Tasted of a Good Fruit, nor a Satisfying Cup of Nuts: beCause they are Deprived of the Better Things in Life, and Especially of those "Beautiful Swanky PALACES!" (A New Concept in Living Habits — Swanky Palaces for Poor People!) By The Worldwide People's Revolution!® Book 066, which everyone could be Living in, and Enjoying 50,000 or more Fruits, Nuts, Vegetables, and Flowers.

05-08 [_] Well, my Enlightened Friend, the Gods are Like those Beautiful Little Rocks, each of which is Different, having Different Sizes, Shapes, and Colors; but, all of them are POLISHED, whereby their Beauty can be Seen, which is WHY that we were Born here, whereby God might get us Polished and Refined, and Bring Out the

Beauty within us; but, only IF we are Like those Gemstones, and not just Ordinary Ugly Gray Shale, or Sandstone, which can also be Beautiful in its own Way; but, never as Beautiful as those Gemstones, each of which is UNIQUE: beCause it is the only one that is Exactly Like it, even as those Marble Tiles that are shown after Verse 03-01, which come from the Mountains, which can be Used Wisely for Decorating the Houses and Palaces that People can Build for themselves, if they Produce the Correct Tools to Work with, instead of making very Expensive Jet Bombers, Army Tanks, Stinking Diesel Trucks, Airplanes, Cars, Pickup Trucks, Motorcycles, Vans, Buses, Lawnmowers, Chainsaws, Cheap Refrigerators, and whatever they Imagine is GOOD for them, when none of those Vain Things are NEEDED. §‡

05-09 [_] So, O Moses, are Cedar Closets Needed? Is that a VAIN Thing of the World, or what?

05-10 [_] No, that is NOT a Vain Thing of the World: beCause it is Useful and Good; but, the Pretty Red Car is NOT Good: beCause it Greatly Pollutes the Air, Water, Land, Plants and Creatures. In Fact, it is nothing but a Grand Deception and Stinking Abomination, for Lazy People!

♦♦♦♦♦♦ — Chapter 06 — ♦♦♦♦♦♦

What are the Vain Things of this World?

06-01 [_] *"Love not the World, neither any of the Vain Things that are in this World: beCause, if any Man Loves the World, the Love of the Heavenly Father is not in him."* — NMV of First John 2:15. *If you were of the World, the People of the World would Love you: beCause they Love their own Kind of People; but, beCause you are not of this World, they Hate you and Despise you: beCause they are Blinded by their False Riches, being Possession Worshipers, like the Ancient Baal Worshipers, who Sold their Souls to Satan to Obtain their Possessions. Nevertheless, I have Chosen you to be my Self-Disciplined Ones, and I have Called you to Come Out of the World, and be Separated from them, and Touch none of their Unclean Things, whereby you might become a Glorious Church, without Pimples, Spots, nor Wrinkles, which can only be Obtained by much Fasting and Praying, even as Moses and Elijah Obtained it, who had their Faithful Servants to Help them to Obtain it: beCause they Purified their Minds and Bodies, which is only Possible by much Fasting and Praying, while Seeking the Government of the Gods, whereby they were Filled with the Holy Spirit, and had the Powers of the Gods to Perform Various Kinds of Miracles, which you can also Obtain, if you have the Faith, Hope, Trust, Love, Patience, Persistence, and OBEDIENCE, which are "The Seven Basic Spiritual Building Blocks of LIFE!" which are Required for being Saved for any Positions within the Holy Kingdom of All that is Good, which is the Government of Jehovah God, who is not a Possession Worshiper; but, that is not to say that he does not have Possessions: beCause, he Possesses everything within this Solar System, which was Given to him by Moklom, who is the Supreme Ruler of this Galaxy, whose Great Golden Throne is Located around Orion, which has an Extremely Beautiful World, which is even more Glorious than Jupiter with its Multitude of Worlds within Concentric Worlds. Howbeit, why would Jehovah God ask you to not Love the World, since he Loved the People of the World so much that he Sacrificed his only Chosen Son, who was Begotten by the Power of the Holy Spirit, which came upon Joseph and Mary while they were Sleeping, whereby the Holy Spirit Transferred the Seed of Adam into the Womb of Mary, whereby I was Conceived and Born into this World, being the same Spirit who was in the Body of Adam, who brought about the Fall of Mankind: beCause of Eating the Forbidden Fruit from the Tree that Represented the Nolij of All that is Good and Evil. Indeed, I was Chosen by our Heavenly Father to Govern this World: beCause I*

Qualified myself in another World of a Higher Order than this World, whereby Yohoovu God Chose me to Govern this World; but, only after being Tested in the Furnace of Afflictions, whereby he might Know for Sure that I would be Faithful to his Divine Laws and Flexible Rules: beCause of Willingly Choosing to Love and Obey him, even as you have Willingly Chosen to Love and Obey me, which is why that I have Chosen you to be my Self-Disciplined Disciples, who must be Contented with Foods and Clothing and whatever Shelters are Provided for you by the People of this World, who Understand the Master Plan of the Master Farmer, who would have all Peoples to Prosper and be in Good Health, which can only be Done, IF you have lots of Good Foods and Natural Drinks to Consume: beCause, you cannot become Holy while Feasting at the Death and Hell Restaurant with the Gluttonous Hogs and Filthy Barking Dogs, who are just Naturally Offended by all such Inspired Words of Provable Truths: beCause, the very same Words that Comfort the Righteous Ones, are the very same Words that Condemn the Guilty Ones, and make them Angry: beCause they are the Adopted Children of Satan, who have Sold their Souls to the Devil, who Seeks their Destruction and Damnation: beCause he Hates our Heavenly Father, and Envies him for his Goodness and Great Riches, who would have all People to be Healthy, Wealthy and WISE; but, the Evil Greedy Selfish People of this World of Woes do not Understand the Master Plan of the Master Farmer, who Believes in Good Humble Masters and Good Obedient Servants, none of whom are Slaves of any Kind: beCause, each Person does his or her Small Part to make the Government of God Function Correctly, even as a Beehive is Managed by a Queen, who has her own Obedient Servants and Drones, who must be Submissive to her, and Cooperative: beCause there is no other Way to Obtain Perfect Peace nor True Prosperity for everyone: beCause no Man can Serve 2 Masters. Indeed, you cannot Serve both God and Materialism, as my Disciples: beCause, in the Process of Serving Materialism, you will Lose your Spiritual GIFTS, which come from the Most-High God, who is a Great SPIRIT BEING, whose Holy Spirit Livz within Holy Temples, only, even though she may Visit Unholy Temples, now and then, just to Teach certain Good Lessons, if any Man can Learn to Tune-in and Listen to her Still Small VOICE, which only Speaks to Innocent People with Pure Minds — such as that Colorful Peacock from Angel Ridge, at King's Mountain, Kentucky 40442 United States of North America, who is the Inspired Author of more than 364 Exceptionally Good Books — speaking of Things to Come, as if they had already Come, as Nephi might say: beCause, all of those Things will Come to Pass during the Last Days, just before my Second Coming: beCause, the Man with the Spirit of Elijah must get everything Straightened Out, before I will Return:

beCause, I must have a True Church to Govern when I Come, who Understand what is Required for Governing this World of Wonders, which Needs True Men of Great Faith, who Attend to the Spiritual Things, who may be called Bishops, Priests, Professors, and Teachers, who must be Contented with Food and Clothing, as I was saying: beCause they do not Want to be Sidetracked by Worldly Ambitions: beCause those are Good Things that can be and should be Attended to by Unholy People, who Know for a Fact that they are not Called to be Kings, Governors, Priests, nor Elected Officials of **"The New RIGHTEOUS One-World Government!" (HOW to Establish a Righteous One-World Government without Going to WAR!) By The Worldwide People's Revolution!®** *Book 056, which must be Established before I will Return: beCause, it is Necessary for those Worldly People to Build* **"The Great World TEMPLE of PEACE!" (The Glory of Jerusalem Arises Again in the Great State of Flexible Texas!) By The Worldwide People's Revolution!®** *Book 017B, which will be the Headquarters for that New Righteous One-World Government, which will have one Great Selected King, who will be Selected by 60 Elected Righteous Kings from 60 Major Nations, and by a Maximum of 600 Elected Righteous Governors from Minor Nations, Provinces and Islands of the Seas, whose Peoples must be Represented within that Great Temple, who may Vote for whatever they Want: beCause they must be Free to Do that, just to Feel like they are a Part of the Government System, even though Voting, itself, has no Power to Accomplish any Good Things: beCause, it is mostly just a Deception of the Mind, as Benjamin Franklin will Explain, who will Understand that Ignorant People must have someone to Blame for whatever goes WRong, after they Elect that Scapegoat to Represent them. Yes, Voting is a Harmless Thing; but, also a Deceptive Thing: beCause, if there is nothing Good to Vote for, it is like Throwing the Dice, which might have Double Sixes or Single Black Dots, only: beCause it is all a Matter of CHANCES. However, when the Masses of People Learn about a Righteous One-World Government, which has an Unlimited Supply of Good Money, which must be EARNED by Honest Labor, they will Cheerfully* **"VOTE for The GOAT!" (The New Political Party that has Guaranteed Solutions for our Massive Problems!) By The Worldwide People's Revolution!®** *Book 109: beCause they Understand that it is much Better if all Righteous People have an Opportunity to Liv within those* **"GLORIOUS Swanky Hotels Castles and Fortresses!" (Beautiful Planned City States for WISE Intelligent Well-Educated People with Common Sense and Good Understanding!) By The Worldwide People's Revolution!®** *Book 019B, which will Solve no less than 5,000 Problems: beCause of Wisely*

Using Elevators, Escalators, and Electric Subway Trains, which are always on Time, never in any Accidents, Spacious, and Comfortable with Swanky Recliners and Easy Chairs to get into and out of, without any Seat Belts: beCause, it is Impossible for such One-Way Trains to CRASH, which will be Managed by **"The Swanky Association of Transportation and Communications,"** *which will be Well-Organized by the Appointed Servants of that Great Selected King, who will have his Cabinet of Secretaries and their Voluntary Servants, who will also be Contented with the Foods and Clothings that are Provided for them by* **"The Swanky Associations of Working Soldiers!" (A Fascinating Collection of Various Kinds of Voluntary Working Soldiers!) By The Worldwide People's Revolution!® Book 018B,** *who will Attend to the Gardening, according to:* "The LUSCIOUS All-Mineral Organic Method of Gardening!" (HOW to Grow DELICIOUS Satisfying Foods for Potential Kingz and Kweenz in Beautiful Swanky PALACES!) By The Worldwide People's Revolution!® **Book 021B,** *which is a Companion Book of:* "Orgimmick Gardening at its Best!" (HOW to Grow Delicious Satisfying Foods without a 10 Million-Dollar Investment!) By The Worldwide People's Revolution!® **Book 079,** *which has more than 60 Photographs with Explanations for Wise People to Study, and especially those who were Born to be MASTERS: beCause, the Perfect Government has both Masters and SERVANTS, which is Explained in:* "A Sound Argument for Good Masters and Obedient Servants!" (WHY Everyone Needs a Good Master, and every Master Needs Good Obedient Servants!) By The Worldwide People's Revolution!® **Book 008B,** *which should be Carefully Studied by all Potential Masters, who can then Explain it to their Voluntary Servants, who must come to Understand that not everyone is Chosen to be a Master. Indeed, most of the People, who were Born to be Masters, who have Extra Brilliant Minds, have simply taken Advantage of those Poor People who were Born to be Servants, and have made them into their Education Slaves, Work Slaves, Tax Slaves, Insurance Slaves, Rent Slaves, Home-owner Slaves, Interest Slaves, Mortgage Slaves, ElecTrickery Bills Slaves, Food Bills Slaves, Water Bills Slaves, Gas Bills Slaves, Transportation Bills Slaves, Repair Bills Slaves, Telephone Bills Slaves, Internet Bills Slaves, Entertainment Bills Slaves, Drug Bills Slaves, Doctor Bills Slaves, Hospital Bills Slaves, Childcare Bills Slaves, Nursing Home Bills Slaves, and Funeral Home Bills Slaves: beCause it is an Edomite Slavery System, which God HATES, and so should every Righteous Person, who should Check the above Check Box with a* LARGE GREEN-X MARK, *just to let everyone Know that they are Honest Trustworthy Masters, who will be Contented with whatever Foods and Clothings are Provided by* **"The Swanky Associations of**

Working Soldiers!" *who are Like the Servants of the Queens in those Beehives, who Keep themselves Busy with Material and Physical Ambitions: beCause, they have nothing Better to Do as Good Servants, whose Master Architects, Engineers and Designers will be Designing the most Beautiful Planned City States in this Solar System, if they set their Minds on it, and put their Bodies to Work on it, whereby Yohoovu God will Look Down from his Great Golden Throne Inside of Jupiter, and say to his Holy Angels:* "When you Good Angels get that New Jerusalem Finished, we will Pray for it to be Moved by the Spirit of the Most-High God into a Renewed Earth, even into the Inside of it, where I will Liv with you: beCause it is a very Special and Beautiful Planned City State, which is a Billion Times more Beautiful than that Old Jerusalem, which has been Washed in Blood several Times; and yet, Sadly to Say, those Jews have still not Learned their Lessons: beCause, they have not Studied, "Good Lessons for Honest Wise Men!" (A Simplistic Plan for Totally Solving the Complicated Problems of Deceived Mankind!) **By The Smarter Professor of Common Sense!** Book 125, *which is an Exceptionally Good Book for them to Study, who will just Naturally Despise this Book: beCause of saying,* "That is NOT the Sixth Book of Moses: beCause Moses never Actually Wrote even one Book: beCause, the Books that are Attributed to him, were not Written by him; but, they were Written by Zealous Priests, who Wanted some Control over the Masses of People, and especially over the Israelites, who were Chosen by YHWH to be his Ministers: beCause, each Tribe had their own Special Calling; and the Tribes of JUDAH, LEVI and JOSEPH were Chosen to Govern all of them, with the Help of Benjamin, who were Chosen to be the WARRIORS, or Chief GUARDS for the other Tribes, who are mostly GAY: beCause they have True Love, even as the Apostle Paul had." *Therefore, that is just the Nature of Things, and no one can Change it; nor should they Want to Change it: beCause, whatever was Done during the Past, is in the Past; but, now we must Deal with the FUTURE, which Requires Godly WISDOM, which will Begin among all Nations by Conducting:* "The GREAT Worldwide TELEVISED Court HEARING!" (That Great Meeting of the Most-Intelligent and Well-Educated Minds!) **By The Worldwide People's Revolution!®** Book 041B, *which will Prove to be the single Most-Interesting Event in World History: beCause of all of the Marvelous Things that will be Presented, and Especially by my Servant JOHN, who is still Alive, and more than 2,000 Years Old! Therefore, do not Despise that Great Day, when the Wise Leaders of all Nations will DEMAND that Great Meeting of the Most-Intelligent and Well-Educated Minds: beCause, as John Wrote in one of his little Epistles,* "I Trust that I will be Seeing you soon, in Person." *Yes, he will be the Joker in the Deck of Government Cards,* *you might say, who will Astound everyone with his Great Nolij! And then, both Moses and Elijah will Suddenly Appear, who will Perform Great Miracles to Amaze the Masses of Ignorant People, who will Cheerfully* "VOTE for The GOAT!" (The New Political Party that has Guaranteed Solutions for our Massive Problems!) By The Worldwide People's Revolution!® Book 109, *who is that Colorful Peacock from Angel Ridge, who is neither a Peacock nor a Goat; but, he is LIKE them in some Ways, and is also Like the Great White Workhorse, who Wrote a Famous Book, called:* **"HOW Working People can PROSPER and Live in PEACE Under the Rulership of a RIGHTEOUS KING!" By The Great White Workhorse!** *Therefore, if you have a Copy of it, you might be able to Sell it as a Collector's Item at some Auction Market for a Million Dollars: beCause, there were only 100 or so of them Produced, in 2 Different Versions for both Masters and Servants; and the one for the Masters is the Spiritual one, which only Masters can Relate with, while the Common Person can Relate with the other one: beCause it is Simple. Therefore, Search for those Exceptionally Good Books, and you will Find them.* †§‡§§

06-02 [_] O Moses, was that Verse 06-01 Written by Saint John, himself; or, by you; or, by your Selected King? After all, you have Managed to get me Greatly Confused, while at the same Time you have also Managed to Enlighten my Mind about a lot of Important Subjects, which should be MAGNIFIED: beCause, it is very Important that we get a GOOD Government Established for Jesus Christ to Inherit, when he Suddenly Returns with tens of thousands of his Holy Ones! †§‡§§

06-03 [_] Well, my Friend, that Verse did not Manage to say much about the Vain Things of this World; but, it did Reveal that there are Basically 2 Kinds of People, who are called *Masters* and *Servants,* who have Need for each other; but, the People, who were Born to be Masters, have simply taken Advantage of the Masses of People, and have made them into their SLAVES, even as they Presently are, which no Sane Person can Rightly Argue Against: beCause, that is the TRUTH of it; and it all Revolves around "The Root Cause for almost all Evils!" (The Strange Things that People Say and Do to Get more Money!) By The Worldwide People's Revolution!® Book 078, which is Magnified by: "For the Love of Money!" (The Strange Things that People Say and Do to Get more Money!) By The Worldwide People's Revolution!® Book 003B, which is DEBUNKED by: "The New MAGNIFIED Version of the Book of ACTS!" (The Understandable Version of the Acts of the Apostles in Plain English!) By The Worldwide People's Revolution!® Book 063, which makes it Perfectly CLEAR concerning what the Vain Things of this World are, and they are NOT God's Marble, Granite, nor Onyx Rocks: beCause, all of those Good Things were Created for us to Richly Enjoy, as the Apostle Paul Wrote, who should have gone into more Details, except that he Trusted me to Do it! †§‡

06-04 [_] §§ O Moses, I can hardly Think of anything so VAIN as that Worthless Onyx Egg and Vase, which have NO GOOD PURPOSE AT ALL! But, if you Think so, please Explain it to me.

06-05 [_] Well, my Friend, I Fully Realize that the Photograph of those Gemstones is an Injustice to them: beCause they are much more Beautiful in Person, when you have them in your Hands. Nevertheless, you can See SOME of the Beauty of them, which is to give to you an Idea concerning what Beautiful Things that God has Prepared for those Wise People, who Love ALL that is GOOD. Therefore, that is WHY that God Provided them for us to Look at. See *First Corinthians 2:9 KJV*. Yes, it is for our Encouragement and Inspiration, which is Required for not making a Big Mess of the entire Earth, such as the Trash Dump that it now is, which you can See above Verse 04-07. †§‡

06-06 [_] O Holy Moses, I can hardly Think of anything so VAIN as that Big Pyramid at Uxmal, Mexico, unless it is an Ugly Mountain of Rocks, which has no Value nor Importance, at all. †§‡§§

06-07 [_] Well, my Poor Ignorant Friend, if you cannot See the Great Beauty of the Mountains, Oceans, Lakes, Rivers, Trees, Flowers, Birds, Wild Animals, Domesticated Animals, and all such Good Things, it is Obvious that you Desperately Need to Do some FASTING, whereby some of the Slime might get Removed from your Cataracts, or whatever is Blinding your Deprived Eyes.‡

The leading causes of blindness and low vision in the United States are primarily **age**-related eye diseases such as **age**-related macular degeneration, cataract, diabetic retinopathy, and **glaucoma**. Other common eye disorders include amblyopia and strabismus.

www.cdc.gov › visionhealth › basics › ced ▾
Common Eye Disorders and Diseases | CDC

06-08 [_] O Moses, it is written that you were 120 Years Old, and your Eyes were not Dim, nor your Sexual Forces Abated, which Means that you were not Sterile; but, Virile, like a Real Stud!‡

06-09 [_] Well, my Friend, it is True that Holy Men are much more Virile than Unholy Men, no matter what their Ages are: beCause the Body of a Holy Man Functions like it should. See *Jobe 33:25, Gay King James V.*

06-10 [_] It might Surprise some People to Learn that Jehovah God is a BODY BUILDER, who Likes to Work with ROCKS, who was one of the Giants, who came to this Earth in his Great Spaceship, many thousands of Years Ago, in Order to Do some Amazing Stonework; but, not on Easter Island: beCause, that was all done by Ambitious Islanders, using Ropes to Guide their Giant Stones, who Rocked and Rolled them on their Bases, whereby they Walked them into their Places.

✦✦✦✦✦✦ — Chapter 07 — ✦✦✦✦✦✦

WHO Set Up Stonehenge?

07-01 [_] Believe it or not, Jehovah God Set Up Stonehenge, just to get People's Attention: beCause, he was and still is one of the GIANTS, who is about 400 feet Tall, who Picked me Up and Placed me in a Cave on the Side of a Mountain, after I Asked him to Show to me all of his Naked Glory: beCause, I wanted to See how Well Equipped he was for Reproducing more Giants, who put me into that Cave just before he Stripped Off his Robe, and put his Hand over the Mouth of that Cave, and then he Walked by, in front of me, before he took his Giant Hand away, and allowed me to See his Backside; but, not his Frontside: beCause, he Clearly said that no Man could See his Face, and Liv to tell about it, which is all Explained in *Exodus 33,* except for the Rest of the Story, which is Actually the Best of it, which those Lying Conniving Edomites did not Like. ‡

07-02 [_] So, O Moses, will you now Tell to us the Rest of the Story, whereby we might Understand just Exactly WHY those Lying Conniving Edomites would DELETE that Precious Part of *Exodus 33,* which must have had something to do with MONEY: beCause, those Edomites would not have Deleted it, unless they stood to Lose some Money for Publishing it, Stark Naked.

07-03 [_] Well, my Friend, considering the Fact that it was Originally my own Story to Tell, and in my own Way, I would like to say that those Edomites had no Right to Alter my Words. However, they Obviously Realized that if they did not Delete Words, and Alter whatever Remained, they would not have a Sellable Book, which is also True of this Inspired Book: beCause, if something Sounds Strange, or just Unbelievable, it usually does not Sell Well, which makes me Hesitate to Publish any such Words, even now: beCause, this Needs to be a Number-one Best-selling Book.‡

07-04 [_] O Holy Moses, when the Man with the Spirit of Elijah Obtains the Power to Transform Rough Rocks into Pure Gold, you will not have to Worry about being Able to Sell any one of his Inspired Books: beCause, they will all Sell like Hotcakes with Maple Syrup on them, and plenty of it: beCause most People are Craving Provable Truths, even if they do not Presently Realize it.‡

07-05 [_] Well, my Friend, you have a Good Point there; but, suppose that he does not Obtain the Power to Transform Mountains of Rough Rocks into Pure Gold? Suppose that Jehovah God comes to Realize that People will be Lusting after that Gold, and will Seek to Re-establish the Old Monetary Edomite Slavery System, whereby only a few People get Excessively Rich, while the Masses of People are made into Education Slaves, Work Slaves, Tax Slaves, Interest Slaves, Credit Card Debt Slaves, Mortgage Bills Slaves, Food Bills Slaves, Water Bills Slaves, ElecTrickery Bills Slaves, Childcare Bills Slaves, Drug Bills Slaves, and all of those other Kinds of Slaves, who are only Mentioned in Verse 06-01? Suppose that God Foresees the Corruption that will Arise among the Children of Unclean Men, who Fail to Understand WHY they were Born into this World: beCause of not taking the Time to Carefully Study Chapter 06, much less, this Inspired Chapter?‡

07-06 [_] O Holy Moses, it would Actually only Require his 98% Rock House at Frog Level to be Transformed into Pure Gold, just to get the Attention of the Masses of "Modern Deceived SLAVES!" (10 Simple Steps for Liberating ALL Modern Slaves, Worldwide, Including Yourself!) **By Liberty and Justice for ALL! Book 113 — except that there is a Great NEED for a LOT of Gold, just to Use it Wisely for making Money, for "The New RIGHTEOUS One-World Government!" (HOW to Establish a Righteous One-World Government without Going to WAR!) By The Worldwide People's Revolution!® Book 056, for Hiring those "Seven Great Armies of Working Soldiers!" (HOW to Provide a Way for Everyone to WORK: so as to Eliminate Poverty, Crimes, Drug Abuses, Prisons and Unnecessary Taxes!) By The Worldwide People's Revolution!® Book 015B, to Build those "GLORIOUS Swanky Hotels Castles and Fortresses!" (Beautiful Planned City States for WISE Intelligent Well-Educated People with Common Sense and Good Understanding!) By The Worldwide People's Revolution!® Book 019B: beCause of Suffering with "Poverty Hunger Riots Strikes Police Brutalities Election Deceptions and Civil Wars!" (The High Price that we Earthlings have Paid for Leaving the Good Land!) By The Worldwide People's Revolution!® Book 014B? §‡**

07-07 [_] ♦ Well, my Friend, this is what the Master Farmer has to say about it, who can Visualize what is Coming — *Listen to me, all of you Modern Deceived Slaves: beCause Provable Truths only Ask for a Fair Hearing, as Moses said. Therefore, Dig Out the Wax of Unbelief from your Spiritual Ears, and Listen to me with your Undivided Attention: beCause, it is Possible and most Practical for all of you to become*

Moderately RICH, just by Electing Righteous KINGS to Govern you: beCause of Establishing "The New RIGHTEOUS One-World Government!" *which can Operate with or without any Money, which is generally just a Waste of Time and Energy to Handle it, and Keep Records of all of it, which a Righteous Government can Liv without — except that the Masses of Ignorant People are Totally Addicted to Using Money, and would hardly Understand HOW that they might Liv without it, and even Raise their Standard of Living by no less than 100 Times, just by Learning, Believing, Loving and Obeying **"The New MAGNIFIED Version of the 20 Commandments,"** which Clearly States that the New Righteous One-World Government should Mint and Print the Necessary New Money for Hiring those Working Soldiers to Help Build those Glorious Swanky Hotels, Castles and Fortresses, which will Represent that New Money, which must be Earned by Honest Labor, according to* "A List of FAIR Swanky Wages!" (The Equitable Wage System!) By The Worldwide People's Revolution!® Book 065, *which will Work Well, if everyone is Perfectly Honest, and does not Try to Cheat the Economic System in any Way; but, puts in 4 Hours of Common Skilled Labor without any Pay, just to Cover all of their Expenses, who should then go Eat at some* "Royal Swanky Buffets!" (The Best Feasts in the Whole World!) By The Worldwide People's Revolution!® Book 103, *and take Off the Remainder of the Day: beCause of being Contented with Food and Clothing, until all of those* "Beautiful Swanky Stone Dome Home COMPLEXES!" (HOW to Build SECURE Tax-proof, Insurance-proof, Self-air-conditioned, Paint-proof, Rot-proof, Termite-proof, Mouse-proof, Fireproof, Tornado-proof, Hurricane-proof, Thief-proof, and BOMB-PROOF Houses!) By The Worldwide People's Revolution!® Book 102, *have been Finished — at which Time all of those Voluntary Working Soldiers can Move into their Stone Dome Homes, for FREE, and Claim them as their Own: beCause they Helped to Build them. Therefore, they can Liv in them until they Die, and the Clouds in the Sky will not Object to it, and neither should any Holy Angels. Therefore, why should anyone else Object to it? After all, every Mountain of Rocks and River of Water Actually Belongs to ME, your Great Creator God, which I could Charge you for, if I were a Greedy Selfish Capitalist HOG; but, I am not. In Fact, I am the Most-Generous God among all of the Gods: beCause, I can Afford to be Generous: beCause, I have the Power to Transform Rocks into Pure Silver and Gold, as well as Gemstones of all Colors and Kinds, which I Intend to Do for my Selected King, just to Prove it to the Boneheads and Hardhearts, who do not even Believe in the Master Farmer and Great Creator God, who Deserve to Suffer with another Black Death, even as they Suffered Centuries Ago: beCause of Eating Unclean Creatures, and* *far too much of whatever they were Eating: beCause, it does not Require as much Food as some Body-builder might Require for Building Up his Big Muscles; but, it does Require Good Wholesome Natural Foods and Drinks to be Healthy, which should be Grown in the Multitude of Terraced Gardens within Swanky Fortresses, just as it is Written: beCause, that is* "The Right Design for Living!" (A List of Great Advantages for Building Beautiful Planned City States!) By The Worldwide People's Revolution!® Book 012B, *which will Produce* "The Environmentalists' Perfect Paradise!" (HOW almost Everyone can be Living in a Beautiful Manmade Paradise!) By The Worldwide People's Revolution!® Book 035C, *for everyone who Believes and Obeys, who has* "The Seven Basic Spiritual Building Blocks of LIFE!" (Faith Hope Trust Love Patience Persistence and Obedience!) By The Worldwide People's Revolution!® Book 036, *which are Necessary for Overcoming all of your Sins, and Especially your Dietary Sins, which are your Chief Sins: beCause they Cause most of the other Sins, including your Lusts for that Filthy Money, which is not a Bad Thing, in itself: beCause, like those Onyx Gemstones, it can be Useful; but, unlike those Onyx Gemstones, Money can be Used to Control People and Manipulate them, and even Destroy them, after making Slaves of them, which the Edomites Discovered thousands of Years Ago, which is WHY that they Carefully Removed many of the Most-Precious Parts of the Holy Bible, and Produced a Book that would Sell Well, rather than Enlighten the Minds of the Masses of Slaves, who might Rebel Against their Evil Empire, and Establish* "The New RIGHTEOUS One-World Government!" *which can Prosper without any Money, at all: beCause a Man can Use a Rock without Buying it, which any Farmer or House Builder Knows for a Fact is the Truth of it: beCause, if his Farm has lots of Squarish Building Stones on it, he can Gather them for making a Stone Wall, or even a hundred Stone Walls, if he is very Ambitious, whereby he can Keep his Livestock within his own Walls. However, in the Righteous Government System, no one Claims any Land for himself to Own: beCause he has no Intentions of Selling it: beCause it will be the Inheritance of his own Children, who may Add their own Stone Walls, Stone Houses, Cisterns, Walk-in Coolers, Ice Houses, Greenhouses, Fruit Tree Houses, or whatever they Want, to Prosper, according to their Faith in it, which will Naturally be Greatly Increased if their Land is Productive, which all Lands should be and can be, if they are Treated Properly, which Requires Special Natural Minerals from Powdered Rocks — such as Volcanic Dust from certain Kinds of Volcanos, which will Fertilize the Ground, which the New Righteous Government would Furnish to everyone, for FREE: beCause of having a Righteous King, who Loves everyone who is Willing and Able to Learn and Work, even if they have some Fake Religion: beCause, that Righteous King Understands that everyone can Change his Mind, if he is Persuaded by Reason and Logic to Do so. However, even if he does not Change his Mind, it is Okay: beCause there are all Kinds of Creatures, who have their own Unique Beliefs, and it does not Bother the Consciences of any of the other Creatures, who Learn to Tolerate them. For Example, there are Fields where Horses, Cattle, Hogs, Sheeps and Goats all Liv Together in Peace with Chickens, Turkeys, Pheasants, Ducks, and whatever might be in that Field, if it is Large Enough, or Spaashous Eenuf for them to be Happy. After all, Horses do not really Like the Smell of Rams nor of Billy Goats: beCause they STINK, while Horses do not Stink, which is WHY that they are my Favorite Animals: beCause they are also very Useful Creatures, as well as very Beautiful Creatures, whose Near Relatives are also Useful and Beautiful in their own Ways, including those Zebras, which cannot be Trusted: beCause they have a Wild Nature that no one has Successfully Civilized, which is also True of the American Bisons, whereby a Bull cannot be Trusted, which is why you must not Turn your Back toward them: beCause they could Gore your Back, just for Doing it: beCause they Believe that you are Infringing on their Territory, which they would Naturally Think about almost any Animal, except for Elks, who Know to Keep a Safe Distance from them, just for Homeland Security, you might say: beCause some Old Bulls might Forget to be Civilized: beCause, their Wild Nature is Embedded within their Hearts and Minds, you might say. Therefore, it is Best to just Take Down all of those Hateful Fences, and let the Buffalos Roam on the Great Plains as they Used to Do, and let the Indians Hunt for them, after they have Multiplied by the Millions: beCause, that was their Way of Life, which was Embedded within their Minds and Hearts, also. After all, almost none of those Indians were Called to be Kings nor Queens; but, only Chiefs of little Tribes, if they were Appointed for anything, who should be left alone to Do whatever they Want to, just as long as it does not Harm anyone: beCause, they Fitted right in with the Natural Ecological System during the 1800s. Therefore, they will soon Adapt to that Lifestyle, once again, if they are given a Chance to Do so, who may Make their Colorful Costumes, and Liv in the Buffalo Tents, and Eat on whatever they Hunt for in the Wilderness: beCause Nature will Keep them Under Control with Sicknesses, Diseases, Natural Disasters, and whatever Happens to them, which is the Way that they Like it. Otherwise, they would Cheerfully Adopt the Swanky Fortress System, and Liv in Peace within their own Beautiful Planned City States. However, they would have to be Trained Properly for Building their "Beautiful Swanky Stone Dome Home COMPLEXES!" because they have no Idea HOW to Build them; but, they can easily Understand WHY:*

beCause those Stone Dome Homes will Heat and Cool themselves, if they are Managed Correctly, without Burning any Gas, Heating Oil, Wood, Coal, Dung, nor anything else. Indeed, it is just a Matter of Discovering HOW, which all Indians have Discovered when they Visited Caves — such as Carlsbad Caverns, in New Mexico, which has a Consistent Temperature the Year Around, which Requires a Coat or Jacket, just to be Comfortable and Happy. However, it is far too Humid for most Things, in spite of being in a Desert, which is not nearly as Humid as the Mammoth Caves in Kentucky, which can Grow Mold and Mushrooms. Therefore, in Order to Prevent that Mold, such Stone Dome Home Complexes should have large Swanky Cisterns under ICE HOUSES, which are Used for Sucking Out the Excess Moisture in each House. Yes, it will Naturally Require a LOT of Difficult Work — except that Mechanical Slaves will be Happy to Do 95% or more of that Difficult Work. Moreover, large Men with Big Muscles will also be Happy to Lift Cut Stones for Building all Kinds of Stone Walls: beCause, that is WHY that they were Created, and Born into this World of Wonders, who were also Generally not Born to be Kings, nor Leaders of any Kind, except in their own Families, which is Okay: beCause, each World only Requires one Great King to Govern **"The New RIGHTEOUS One-World Government!"** *which does not Micro-manage each Person, as some Tyrant might Try to Do; but, it Helps all of the People to Prosper, whose Primary Function is to make Sure that everyone gets to Liv within one or the other of those* **"GLORIOUS Swanky Hotels Castles and Fortresses!"** *which should be Built in a Million Different Ways, just to Discover which Kind is Best for Wise People of each Religious and Political Order: beCause, there is no Way in this World that everyone is going to Decide to Adopt the ONE and ONLY True Religion, which is Holiness of Mind, Spirit and BODY, which Requires a LOT of Fasting and Praying and Eating Wholesome Natural Foods and Drinks for Mankind: beCause, People are NOT Cows, Dogs, Hogs, nor Horses; but, they are People, many of whom came from other Worlds, being Transported over here by the Giants of Ancient Times, who brought the Black and Brown Peoples for their Slaves: beCause the Giants were all White Peoples, except for a few Tribes of them, who are now Living Inside of Mars, which is also Hollow, and a Paradise on the Inside of it, even as almost all of the Planets in the entire Universe are Hollow, if they have Moons around them, which were Born from them, which you do not have to Believe to be Saved for another Life in this World: beCause, your Faith in it is not Required for Living another Life; but, you might find it Interesting that your own World has several Kinds of GIANTS Living on the Inside of it: beCause they are not the Barbarians that those Lying Conniving Edomites are, who just Naturally Envy them* *for several Reasons; but, mostly beCause they have Learned how to Prosper without the Use of any Money, which is just a Joke to them: beCause they are not so Stupid as to not be Able to See that the Mountains of Rocks are FREE, along with the Rainwater and Sunlight. Therefore, why not just Manage it Correctly, and take Advantage of those Mountains of Rocks, which have some really Beautiful Stones within them, which only Need to be Cut and Polished? Therefore, when the Masses of People come to their Riit Senses, after Suffering under the TYRANNY of the Edomites for thousands of Years, they will Learn to Work Together like True Brothers and Sisters, if they ever get Converted to the TRUTH, the Whole Truth, and nothing but the Whole Truth, which has nothing for Sale: beCause it has been Liberated from the Prison of Capitalist Lies. Therefore, why Try to Fight Against* "The Swanky Sword of Divine Truths!" (The Most-Powerful Weapon in the Whole Universe!) By The Worldwide People's Revolution!® Book 067? *Why not Humbly Submit to it, and Learn HOW to Cooperate with one another, with True Love for one another, just as if you Lived on a Big Farm that has LOTS of Rocks to Work with, along with everything else that you might Need, without Wasting anything? Indeed, there is no Need for Filling Up the Oceans with your Capitalist Trash, just to make a few Rich Hogs Richer, while making an Ugly World for everyone to Liv in. Therefore, Meditate on it, until you See the Perfect Vision for what is Required, O Sheeple.* †§‡§§

07-08 |_| *First of all, you must do your Best to make Perfect Copies of this Inspired Book — not to Sell to anyone; but, to be Generous and GIVE them to whomever Wants to Reed them, and Promises to Reed them, Carefully, and make Check Marks or X-Marks in the Appropriate Boxes: beCause of Agreeing or Disagreeing with the Statements, which will Help them to THINK, and which will also Require a little "Missionary Work," you might say, which Requires a little Wisdom, which not everyone has; but, most People do have it, who can simply say to their Naaberz: "I was given this Book, which I would like you to Read, and let me know what you Think of it: beCause, I just Want your Honest Opinion about it, which might Help me to Judge its Goodness. After all, why would anyone Give to me such an Expensive Book, if they did not Love my Soul?" And then hand a Clean Copy to them, and say: "If you do not Like it, please give it back to me: beCause, I am Sure that I can Discover other People, who will Appreciate it: beCause, it Reveals HOW we can all get Moderately RICH, without Telling any Lies, nor Selling any Capitalist Trash." And then Smile at them, and say: "Do you Promise to Reed it, or not?" And if that Person says, "Yes, I Promise to Read it," then you have Won a New Friend: beCause, if he were a Bad*

Person, he would Naturally be Offended by your Phrase, "… without Telling any Lies, nor Selling any Capitalist Trash," beCause, he or she might be another Capitalist, who has been Sold Down the River with Poor Nigger Jim, into Eternal Slavery, and does not even Realize it: beCause, he or she does not Know what a True Slave is, nor how he or she was Made into one, who is so Deceived that he or she does not even Realize that he or she is a Work Slave, Tax Slave, Insurance Slave, Interest Slave, Credit Card Debt Bills Slave, Food Bills Slave, Water Bills Slave, Gas Bills Slave, Drug Bills Slave, nor one of those other Kinds of Slaves, which are Mentioned in Verse 07-07. Indeed, you really do not have to Say anything, except to Open up this Book to this Paragraph, and say: "Would you mind reading this, and explaining to me what this might Mean?" while Pointing to this Verse, at which Time that Person will say something like this, "What do we have here?" or "What do you have there?" or "Let me reed it." Indeed, if they seem to be Skeptical, you can say: "You Look like an Intelligent Person. Therefore, would you Mind Reeding this Paragraph, and tell me what it Means?" at which Time he or she might say, "No, I do not mind it." And then, when they get finished with it, they will say something like this: "You know full well what it is saying, and so do I. Therefore, why did you Ask me to Reed it?" And you can say, "Well, I just had to Discover whether or not you Like to Reed Inspired Books." And they will say, "What Business is it of yours?" or, "What makes you Imagine that it is an Inspired Book?" at which Time you can say, "Well, if you Doubt it, just Reed Verse 07-07, and you will have no more Doubts," at which Time they will say something like this, "I do not have Time for any such Nonsense — I have Things to Do," which you can Respond to, by saying: "So, it is True, you are just another Self-Deceived SLAVE, just as Verse 07-07 states in so many Words," and they will say, "I am NOT a Slave, nor do I like your False Accusations: beCause I am Free, and can Do whatever I Want to Do: beCause I am an American, and Proud of it," to which you can Respond, saying: "If you are Truly Free, how come you do not have enough Time to reed Verse 07-07? I have Red it no less than 10 Times, and the more often that I Reed it, the Better it gets: beCause all Inspired Books are like that," at which Time he or she will say, "Well, to each his own — go Reed it again; but, leave me alone: beCause, I am not at all Interested in it," to which you may Respond, saying: "Are you saying that you are not Interested in becoming Moderately RICH, without Selling anything?" to which he or she will Respond, "It is probably another Capitalist HOAX to get my Money," to which you can Reply, "If you Promise to Reed this Book, you can have it for Free: beCause I am Giving it to you," to which he or she will Reply, "Okay, I Promise to Reed it; but, if I do not Like it, I will give it back to you, or *else put it into the Trash Can," to which you must Reply, "That would be a Major Sin: beCause this Inspired Book was Given to us by the Master Farmer, who might be Offended if it were Trashed," to which he or she might say: "Who in Hell is the Master Farmer?" to which you can Respond, by saying: "Why are you suddenly Angry? Have you never Met the Master Farmer? That is Jesus Christ," to which he or she might say: "And how did you Meet him?" to whom you can Answer, "I Met him by Reeding this Inspired Book, which Instructed me to Repent of all of my Sins, and to Beg God to Forgive me in the Name of Jesus Christ," to which he or she might say: "I have already Done all of that, and I am Saved and going to Heaven when I Die!" to which you can Respond, saying: "Well then, you will Love this Inspired Book: beCause you have had a Great Change of Mind and Heart, and are now Ready for the Next Step in the Process of your Salvation, which is to be Saved for some Position in the Government of God, which is called the Kingdom of God: beCause it is not a DUMBmocracy; but, it is a Holy KINGDOM, with a Great King in Charge of it, who has a Special World for you to Inherit, if he Finds you Worthy of it," to which he or she might say: "What do you Mean? Are you saying that there are more Worlds, other than this one?" to which you may Respond, "Yes, there are Countless Worlds: beCause the Gods are in the Business of Creating more and more Worlds, to be Inhabited by more and more Peoples: beCause everything is in the Business of Multiplying, just in case you have not Noticed it, including the Creation of New Worlds, which Scientists Confess is True: beCause they have Seen New Stars being Born in their Telescopes. Therefore, would you Like to Inherit your very own World to Govern, even as Jesus Christ Inherited this World?" to which he or she may say, "There is no Way in the World that I could Qualify for that Job: beCause I am too Ignorant," to which you may say, "Well, that is a Good Reason to Study this Inspired Book, which Tells HOW to have a GOOD GOVERNMENT, which is what we Desperately Need, right now," to which he or she may say: "There is no Way to Establish such a Good Government, which would have to be a New RIGHTEOUS One-World Government, just to get some Control over the Pollution and Production of Capitalist Trash: beCause, as of right now, no one is in Control," to which you may Respond: "That is WHY that we Need to Elect a RIGHTEOUS KING to Govern it, who is Granted the Power to Enforce the Laws that we, the People, VOTE for: beCause of Understanding that it is not Good to Fill Up the Oceans with Capitalist TRASH, which Looks really UGLY, if you take a Tourist Boat to See the World, while Floating around in an Ocean of TRASH," to which he or she may Respond, by saying something like this: "I do not have to take a World Tour to See what a Messed Up World this is: beCause, I only Need to Watch the*

Evening Snooze Reports on TV, to Know that this World is in one Hell of a Mess, and the Bug-19 is only making it Worse," to which you may Respond, by saying: "Do you Know how to get Rid of that Bug?" to which he or she might say, "The Medical Doctors are Working on a Vaccine to Cure it," to which you may say, "You Mean to PREVENT it, not Cure it, right?" to which he or she may say, "Yes, I Mean to Prevent it: beCause no one Knows how to Cure it," to which you may say: "But, that is not True: beCause God Knows how to Cure it. In Fact, Jesus went about Healing Diseased People, according to the Holy Bible. Do you not Believe the Holy Bible?" to which he or she might say, "I am not Sure what to Believe, are you?" to which you may say: "Well, that is WHY that you should Reed Verse 07-07, which Reveals HOW to Solve that Problem, which is called 'The Great Worldwide Televised Court Hearing!' (That Great Meeting of the Most-Intelligent and Well-Educated Minds!) By The Worldwide People's Revolution!, which you can Join, yourself, for Free!" to which he or she might say, "I already have Enough Problems, without Joining any Religious Group of Ignorant Fools," to which you may Respond: "They are just Normal People, much like yourself, who have no Idea HOW to Cure the Bug Problem; but, I Know: beCause, I Learned it from Reeding this Inspired Book, which has a Guaranteed Solution for it, which is to Fast and Pray, until it goes Away: beCause that is Nature's one and only Cure for whatever Ails us, which has Worked Well for all of the Wild Animals for Millions of Years: beCause, they have no Hands to Earn any Money, nor any Money for Buying any Drugs, nor Medical Services: beCause they Understand that every Body was made to Heal itself, and without the Assistance of any Medical Snakes: beCause, when you Lose your Appetite, that is a Sign to STOP EATING, which is a Good Thing: beCause it gives the Body Time to Repair itself, and Build Up an Immunity to any and all Diseases, which it begins to do, right away, within 3 to 4 Days, if you just give it a Chance to Do what it Wants to Do: beCause the Body is Smarter than you Think. Therefore, if we Cooperate with it, it will Heal itself, and especially if we Earnestly Pray to God, in the Name of our Anointed Savior, who will Help us to get Well: beCause he Promised to Do so, which you can Prove, just by Doing it; but, you have to be Free to Do it, and not be a Slave of any Kind, which is the Reason for having a Church, which can Help you to Do it, even as Joshua Helped Moses, and Elisha Helped Elijah, and the Holy Angels Helped Jesus: beCause, it is very Difficult for a Sick Person to go get a Gallon of Fresh Orange Juice, for Example, when it is Time to FLUSH OUT his Bowels, along with all of the Accumulated Poisons and Stinking Filth within the Bowels, which is what is making that Person SICK, which is a Great Relief, just to get RID of it, which makes a Person Feel

Really GOOD the next Day, after all of those Stinking Poisons have been Flushed Down the Toilet," to which he or she may Respond: "Yes, I Remember the last Time that I got Sick, and Vomited Out Gallons of Stinking Filth, and also got a Diarrhea, whereby I Passed Out more Gallons of Stinking Poisonous Filth, which had Accumulated within my Bowels, which made me Feel Really GOOD when it all got Out of me. Therefore, that Sickness Saved my Life: beCause, if that Poisonous Filth had Remained within me, it might have Killed me! Therefore, I should Thank God for getting Sick: beCause it was a Good Thing, which Saved my Life!" to which you may Respond: "Yes, that is True for everyone who gets Sick, and Vomits and Pukes and gets a Diarrhea, which is an Internal House-cleaning, which generally Happens to People once or twice per Year, if they are fairly Healthy; but, if you do not Like it, just Stop Eating with the Dogs and Hogs," at which Time he or she might be Offended and Defensive, saying: "I do not Eat with the Dogs, nor with the Hogs — are you Suggesting that my Family and Friends are Dogs and Hogs?" at which Time you may say: "No, it is just a Figure of Speech, which should not Offend you, if you are a True Christian: beCause, at certain Times — such as Thanksgiving and Christmas — we all Eat too much, which Causes most of us to get Sick in January: beCause it is Cold, and our Bodies CONTRACT, which Forces some of the Accumulated Filth Out of our Muscles, and into our Bloodstreams, which is then Deposited into our Bowels, whereby it might be Deposited into the Toilet: beCause our Bodies must get Rid of it, just to Save our Lives from all of those Accumulated Poisons, which may Drain Out of our Nostrils, Ears, Eyes, Sores, Wounds, or Pores of our Skins by Sweating with a Fever. Therefore, we should be Thankful that God has made our Bodies in such a Way as to have Internal House-cleaning Days. Therefore, after the Vomiting and Diarrhea, we must Remember to NOT PUT ANY MORE DOG FOODS nor HOG SLOP into our Stomachs, lest we should Repeat the same Sickness, or even Contract some Hateful Disease. For Example, if the Body cannot get Rid of those Poisons by Vomiting and Diarrheas, it will Store Up those Poisons in Lumps, in Boils, in Tumors, and in Abscesses in our Livers: beCause, the Body must Deal with it, somehow, until it gets an Opportunity to get Rid of it. However, if it cannot get Rid of it, a Good Thing called CANCER will Attack it, and Eat on it, and Try to get Rid of it. Therefore, when a Red Spot shows up on your Skin, that is a Warning Sign that Cancer is at Work within your Body, somewhere, which Means that it is Time to FAST and PRAY, in Order to give the Body an Opportunity to Cleanse itself, by SQUEEZING OUT any Unwanted Accumulated Filth, which can be Assisted by Drinking Fresh Fruit Juices; or, just by Eating mostly Fruits and Laxative Vegetables — such as Red Garden Beets, Spinach,

Kale, Fresh Green Onions, Raw Cabbages, Cole Slaw, Squashes, Cucumbers, Pickles, Melons, Watermelons, Grapes, Berries, and whatever is LAXATIVE, which might have a Chance of going through the Pipes of the Bowels, where Lumps and Filth have Accumulated, whereby some Ignorant People Weigh a hundred or even 200 Pounds too much, who look Pregnant with Lumps and Tumors on the Insides of them, who are called Dietary Sinners, who are most often not even Aware of how Badly that they are Mistreating themselves by EATING, which they Imagine is Necessary for SURVIVAL, when just the Opposite is the Case, which Moses Proved when he went up on Mount Sinai, and Fasted and Prayed for 40 Consecutive Nights and Days, when he was 80 Years Old, and twice in a Row, until he became a Holy Man, who was Cleansed from ALL Accumulated Internal FILTH, which STINKS: beCause it is Old Rotten Morbid Matter, which Great Truth the Doctor Niif has yet to Discover: beCause, in spite of having a Nose, he cannot Smell Out the Truth of it: beCause God has Blinded his Mind, whereby he cannot Understand the most Simple Truths: beCause he is Blinded by his PRIDE, which Prevents him from Escaping from his Dark Loathsome Prison of Traditional Lies, which he was Born into, which has only one Way Out of it, which is to Pass Through the Doorway of CONFESSION! But, being so Proud of himself for getting such a Good Education with a Capital G and E, as in General ElecTrickery, he is Destined for the Sanitized Slaughterhouse, where they Remove Precious Million-dollar Organs with 10-cent Razorblades, you might say, without Realizing what Great Damages that they are Doing to the TEMPLE of GOD, called a Human Body, which does not Like being Mistreated so Cruelly and Meanly, which only Asks for a BREAK, or TIME-OUT, when it can get Sick, and Vomit Out some of that Filth and Poisons; but, the Doctor Kaaoopektaat, and the Doctor Peptoobizmuk Sincerely Believe that all of that Poison should Remain within the Victim of Capitalism: beCause they Juj that Sicknesses and Diseases are BAD Things, when they are Actually very GOOD Things: beCause they are Saving People's Lives; but, only if they Listen to their PAINS, which are Warning Signs that something is Terribly WRong within the Bowels and Body of the Ignorant Victim of Vain Traditions, who must Humble himself, and Confess ALL of his Sins, just to be Enlightened and Saved from them: beCause, Crying Helps the Body to Save itself, and Especially if it is DEEP MOURNFUL Crying, Weeping and WAILING, just as the Apostle said — 'Let your Laughter be Turned into Mourning, and your Rejoicing into Heaviness, like a Weary Man, who has Carried a Heavy Load of Accumulated Filth for 40 Years, and Seeks to be Free from it; and Humble yourself by Means of Fasting and Praying, whereby you might be Saved' — except that those Lying Conniving Edomites REMOVED that Part from the

Scriptures: beCause they did not Want their Slaves to Realize the GOODNESS of Fasting nor Praying, and Especially when it is Combined with certain Days of Feasting on Sweet Juicy Fruits, which Help to Dissolve and Eliminate all of that Sticky, Gooey, Gummy PASTRIES, Pizzas, Pies, Puddings, Cakes, Cookies, Candies, Cheeses, Iced-creams, and other STICKY STUFFINGS, Dressings, JAMS, Jellies, Eggnogs, French-fried Potatoes, Greasy Hamburgers, and whatever might be Difficult to Run THROUGH a one-inch PIPE that is 26 feet Long, which has no Hot Water, Soap, nor Scrub Brushes to Help WASH IT OUT; BUT, it does have some Fruit Juices to Soften it up, and Sweep it Out with Cole Slaw, which is made without Maaunaaz: beCause it contains Eggs and Oil, which are also STICKY, which Stick in Frying Pans, for Example, while Painters, like Michelangelo and Leonardo da Vinci used Egg Whites to Smear onto Canvases: beCause, when Raw Egg Whites get Spread Out and Dried Out, they make the Perfect GLUE to Paint on, which can Stick there for thousands of Years! Likewise, Beef Broth can be Boiled Down, to make GLUE for Gluing Furniture Together: beCause, it is very STICKY STUFF, you might say, which Sticks in the Sinuses, until someone Catches a Cold, and then the Sinuses Drain Out of the Nostrils and into the Throat, which is the Body's Way of getting Rid of it; but, the Dietary Sinner just Assumes that a Cold or Flu is a BAD THING, which must be Prevented at all Costs: beCause it makes a Person Feel BAD. However, if the Person did not Feel Bad, he might Assume that he is Healthy, Wealthy, and WISE, when he is Actually just another Ignorant FOOL, who is Blinded by PRIDE, who could never Humble himself with King David, nor Confess that he Needs to Study Verse 07-07, which gives the Best Solution for Solving all such Problems," at which Time he or she might say: "I Hear what you are Saying; but, I do not have Time to Fast nor Pray with Moses nor Elijah on Mount Horrible: beCause I have to get to WORK, just to Pay my Endless Bills: beCause, I do not have a True Christian Church to Help me to Do my Fasting nor Praying, except on Sundays, which is the Lord's Day, who said in Matthew 12 that he would be in the Grave for 3 Nights and 3 Days: beCause he was Crucified on Friday, and Buried at Sunset, which was the First Day: beCause Jewish Days BEGAN at SUNSET. Therefore, Friday Night began the First Day, and Easter Sunday Morning Ended the Second Day, and Moonday, at Sunset, was when the 3 Nights and 3 Days Ended, which any little Child could Count; but, not those Wicked Scribes nor Spiritually-blind Pharisees, who cannot even Count 3 Jewish Nights and 3 Jewish Days from Friday Night to Sunday Morning: beCause, they do not Exist! Indeed, at the very Most, there are only 2 Nights and ONE Day, which is Saturn Day. Yes, Friday, or Venus Day is the Jewish Preparation Day for the Seventh-day Sabbath, on

Saturn Day, which Ends at Sunset on Saturn Day, which is just ONE Jewish Day, from Friday Night at Sunset, until Saturday Sunset; and then another Jewish Day Begins, which Ends at Sunset on SUN Day, which is the First Day of the Week to us Pagans, who do not Believe in the Teachings of Moses: beCause he was just plain STUPID, who did not Know that Jesus would be Crucified on a WEDDING Day, called Wednesday, whereby he would be Buried at Sunset, which Began the HIGH Sabbath Day, called the Passover, which fell on a THURSDAY during that Year. Therefore, Jesus was in the Grave from Wednesday Night, until Saturday Night, at which Time he Arose from the Dead, and went to NBC, in New Yuck City, and Attended Saturday Night LIVE with Jay Leno and Mark Twain, who were Discussing the Christian Comedy about the Resurrection of a HOAX! Yes, if Jesus Christ was not a Liar in Matthew 12:40, then he must have been in the Grave from Wednesday Night to Saturday Night: beCause, those are the only 3 Nights and 3 Days that one can Count: beCause there are no 3 Nights nor 3 Days from Friday Night to Sunday Morning! In Fact, my Boss will give to you a Million Dollars CASH, if you can Count 3 Nights and 3 Jewish Days between Friday Night and Sunday Morning: beCause, it does not EXIST — except in the Minds of Ignorant FOOLS, who will look rather Sheepish during the Day of Judgment, when Jesus says: 'Why did you not Believe what I said? Jonah was in the Belly of the Whale Shark for 3 Nights and 3 Whole Days, when he was at last Vomited Out onto Dry Land, who was Sick to his Stomach, after Eating the Rotting Fishes in the Stomach of the Whale Shark; but, that Part of the Story was Carefully Removed by those Lying Conniving Edomites, who did not Want anyone to Discover the Whole Truth, which Jonah Revealed to the People of Nineveh, in a very Long Sermon, which can be found in: "The Gospel According to our Elected King!" (The Good News from the Most Modern Perspective!) By The Worldwide People's Revolution!® Book 077, *who is the Man with the Spirit of Elijah, which you do not have to Believe to be Saved for a Position in the Government of God; but, it Helps to Believe it: beCause his Inspired Books Unravel many Great Mysteries, and Reveal what is Required for Salvation in the Kingdom of God, which Begins with Holiness of Mind, Spirit and BODY: beCause, no Unclean Hogs, Highly-Perfumed Stinking Skunks, Poisonous Snakes, nor Barking Dogs will Enter into that Holy Kingdom,' to which you will have to Confess that you are not Worthy to Enter through those Pearly White Gates, which Symbolize that Holiness of Mind, Spirit and BODY, which must be Cleansed from ALL Unrighteousness, including the Unrightness of Believing Traditional Religious LIES — such as that Easter Sunrise Resurrection Nonsense,' to which you will say, 'O Lordy, I iz jus' unuther Ignernt Ideeut, who shoud hav Studeed Vers 07-07.' Yes, it will Prove to be very Em-bare-assing, you might say, during the Day of Jujmunt, when all of the Inspired Books are Opened, and you have to Explain yourself," to which you may Respond, by saying: "There is only ONE Rational Solution for Solving all of those Religious Disputations, and that is for us Believers to DEMAND:* **'The GREAT Worldwide TELEVISED Court HEARING,'** *whereby we might Learn the Whole Truth, and nothing but the Whole Truth," at which Time he or she might say: "And what is the Great Worldwide Televised Court Hearing? How come we have never Heard about it on the News Broadcasts, nor even on C-SPAN? How come some CONgress Person has not Mentioned it? Why was it not the Number-one Best-selling Book in America? Why is it not Found in every Public LIE-brary? Why is it not Found in every Book Store, and Magazine Rack? Why is it not Displayed at the Check-out Counters at Super Small-mart? Why is this Book not also Found there?" at which Time you may say, "All such Provable Truths might Cause the Customers to Vomit on the Heads of those Lying Conniving Edomites, who cannot Defeat* 'The Swanky Sword of Divine Truths!' (The Most-Powerful Weapon in the Whole Universe!) By The Worldwide People's Revolution!® Book 067: *beCause,* "All of the Arguments are in Favor of our Selected King, who has Zero Challengers!" (Before you Attend another Election Deception, you should Carefully Study this Inspired Book with an Honest Open Mind!) By The Worldwide People's Revolution!® Book 085." And then a Pretty little Red Robbin might Chirp: "Is that the End of an Endless Conversation?" at which Time God might say: "No, I have not even Begun to Speak." §§

07-09 |_] So, my Friends, this Chapter is Long Enough, and that Long Conversation was Long Enough for that Stranger to have Carefully Red ALL of Verse 07-07; but, now that he or she Wasted all of that Time, and got to Work Late, and got Fired for it, and Lost his or her Slave-labor Paycheck, he or she is Ready to Commit SUICIDE! But, Hold everything, and Use your Head to THINK: beCause, there is a Way Out of it, which is to DEMAND: "The GREAT Worldwide TELEVISED Court HEARING!" (That Great Meeting of the Most-Intelligent and Well-Educated Minds!) By The Worldwide People's Revolution!® Book 041B, whereby our Selected King can Ask a few Important Questions, which are Revealed in: "Good Lessons for Honest Wise Men!" (A Simplistic Plan for Totally Solving the Complicated Problems of Deceived Mankind!) **By** The Smarter Professor of Common Sense! Book 125, which should also be Passed Out on the Streets of Sin City, for Free, by "Seven Great Armies of Working Soldiers!" (HOW to Provide a Way for Everyone to WORK: so as to Eliminate Poverty, Crimes, Drug Abuses, Prisons and Unnecessary Taxes!) By The Worldwide People's Revolution!® Book 015B, who have nothing Better to Do, than to Study all such Inspired Books.

07-10 [_] O Holy Moses, how about giving to us some Good Lessons about Managing a RIGHTEOUS One-World Government, without Going to WAR? After all, this is just a Short Book, which Needs some more Pages of Information, whereby a Reader might Spend an Entire Day Reeding it, while Fasting and Praying, which should also be Found in an Audio Format, who would not Dare to Eat any Raw Green Onions to Break his Fast on: beCause, it might give to him Chronic Indigestion, unless they were Chopped Up with Finely-ground Cabbage, Shredded Carrots, Chopped Bell Peppers, Raw Spinach, a few Olives, and some Lime Juice for Dressing. †§‡§§

— Chapter 08 —

HOW to Avoid a Lot of Foolish Arguments

08-01 [_] First of all, it is Most-Important to Discover the Most-Intelligent and Well-Educated People, be they Men or Womb-men, Children or LBGTQ whatever: beCause it is Important to have all of the Facts Lined Up. For Example, we now Know that Ancient Roman Concrete was about 7 Times as Strong as Modern Concrete: beCause the Romans Discovered the Usefulness of Volcanic Dust and whatever was Required for making it Correctly, whereby it would Endure the Test of Time, which we might be able to Improve on, if we Try our Best to Do it. Moreover, the Romans used Fresh Cement to make their Concrete, which was the Primary "Secret" to their Success: beCause, Fresh Cement is much Stickier than Old Cement. In Fact, Modern Cement has Added Chemicals to make it have a Longer "Shelf-Life," and also to make it Deteriorate within 40 Years: beCause, Capitalists want it that Way, whereby they can Sell more Cement for making more Concrete, which is WHY Ballparks are Demolished every 40 Years, or so: beCause the Concrete has Deteriorated, and Needs to be Replaced: beCause that is how the Capitalists Designed it, for PROFIT: beCause, almost everything is Done for PROFIT, for the Capitalist HOGS. †§‡§§

08-02A [_] Please Notice the MUD in that Pile of Gravel. My Brother Vern and I had to Wash 50 Dump Truckloads of that Dirty Gravel, just to get the Mud Removed from it, for Building our Million-dollar Retirement Home: beCause, Cement does not Stick to Mud, which makes very Poor Concrete, which Crumbles and goes to "Hell," as Vern might say, within only a few Years, when it should Endure for at least a thousand Years. {**FOOTNOTE 03.** That Muddy Concrete is what the Federal Government uses for whatever they Produce for their Extremely Poor Tax Slaves: beCause, they do not Care what the Cost is, nor how many Times something Needs to be Replaced: beCause, they are Typical IGNORANT Government Officials, who are often "Career Politicians," who never did an Honest-day's Work during their entire Lives, who are Elected by Typical IGNORANT Uneducated Insurance Slaves, who say: "I will be Dead and Gone when that Concrete goes to Hell. Therefore, what do I Care?" Well, it is for Certain that they do not give a Damn about their own Grandchildren, who will have to Pay the Endless Bills for their Grandparent's Stupidity, who are likely to CURSE them for it: beCause of not making Sure that they Voted for **"The New RIGHTEOUS One-World Government!" (HOW to Establish a Righteous One-World Government without Going to WAR!) By The Worldwide People's Revolution!® Book 056,** which would be Responsible for Doing all such Things CORRECTLY, no matter what the Costs might be, as if Doing those Things for GOD, and not for Corporations, nor for Greedy Selfish Low-life Sons of Satan, who should be Dispatched to HELL, to Liv with their Evil Stepfather. §‡}

The Basics. The Capitol Dome was constructed with **8,909,200 pounds** of ironwork bolted together in a masterpiece of American will and ingenuity. The U.S. Capitol's dome made of cast iron was designed by Thomas U. Walter and constructed from 1856-1866 at the total cost of **$1,047,291**.

www.aoc.gov › buildings-grounds › capitol-dome ▾

Capitol Dome | Architect of the Capitol

Additional stairs lead up into the statue for maintenance. Restoration and conservation of the **Capitol Dome's** cantilevered peristyle and skirting occurred in 2012. In 2013, the Architect of the **Capitol** announced a tentative four-year, $10 million project to **repair** and conserve the **Capitol dome**.

en.wikipedia.org › wiki › United_States_Capitol_dome ▾

United States Capitol dome - Wikipedia

{**FOOTNOTE 04.** So, the Actual Cost of Repairing the Dome on the
Capitol Building was roughly about 56.8 Times the Original Cost of
1,047,291$, which is a long ways from the Original Estimated Cost of
only 10 Million Dollars, which was an Underestimated Cost, which is
True for most everything that the Federal Government does, like the
War in Iraq, which was going to be "a Slam Dunk," according to
George Tenet, which turned out to Cost Trillions of Dollars, and never
got Wrapped Up: beCause, the Terrorist Attacks are still Happening!
†§‡}

Her right hand rests upon the hilt of a sheathed sword wrapped in a scarf; in her left hand she holds a laurel wreath of victory and the shield of the United States with 13 stripes. The helmet is encircled by **nine stars**.

www.aoc.gov › art › other-statues › statue-freedom

The Statue of Freedom | Architect of the Capitol

www.aoc.gov › explore-capitol-campus › art › statue-fr... ▾

The Statue of Freedom | Architect of the Capitol

The helmet is encircled by **nine stars**. ... **Statue of Freedom does** not wear or hold a knitted liberty cap, as **would** have been expected in ... cap encircled with stars, holding a shield, wreath, and sword, which he said **represented** Armed Liberty.

The **Statue of Freedom's** crested helmet and **sword**, suggesting she **is** prepared to protect the nation, **are** more commonly associated with Minerva or Bellona, Roman goddesses of war. The history of the **statue's** design explains why she wears a helmet rather than a liberty cap.

www.aoc.gov › art › other-statues › statue-freedom

The Statue of Freedom | Architect of the Capitol

Statue of Freedom does not wear or hold a knitted liberty cap, as **would** have been expected in nineteenth-century art. The knit cap provided to freed slaves in ancient Rome had been adopted as the **symbol of** liberty or **freedom** during the American and French Revolutions and was usually shown as red.

www.aoc.gov › art › other-statues › statue-freedom

The Statue of Freedom | Architect of the Capitol

What does the Capitol building dome symbolize?

In the 1850s, major extensions to the North and South ends of the **Capitol** were authorized because of the great westward expansion of our nation and the resultant growth of Congress. Since that time, the U.S. **Capitol** and its stately **dome** have become international symbols of our representative democracy.

www.visitthecapitol.gov › about-capitol

About The Capitol | U.S. Capitol Visitor Center

{**FOOTNOTE 05.** A more Appropriate Symbol of Freedom in the Form of a Living Creature, would be a Great Bald Eagle, or a Wild Mountain Sheep, who Lives in Peace, who only Butts Heads with other Wild Mountain Sheeps to Discover WHO is the Boss, which seems to have Worked quite Well for thousands of Years, and is still Working Well. It is a Mystery as to WHY a Woman with a Helmet on her Head, and a Sword in her Hand, was Chosen to Represent Freedom, when she would be the Least Capable of Providing True Freedom, who is most often Responsible for making her Husband and Children so FAT, and Driving him to Drinking by Demanding more Money than he can

Provide with a Low-paying Capitalist Job as a Normal American Work Slave and Tax Slave. Jesus said, *"You shall Learn the Truth, and the Whole Truth will make you Free when you Practice it.,"* which makes the Most Sense to me. What do you Think? Are American Slaves Free in any Way, at all? Well, they are Free to Pay their Endless Bills, and Consume their Countless Pills; but, they are not Free to "VOTE for The GOAT!" (The New Political Party that has Guaranteed Solutions for our Massive Problems!) By The Worldwide People's Revolution!® Book 109. In Fact, they will never See his Name on any Ballot: beCause the Slave Masters do not Want their Slaves to be Freed, which would not be Difficult to Prove in any Courtroom; but, Congress is not Interested in Proving any Truths: beCause, in so Doing, they would put themselves OUT of Business, which would be Bad for Business; but, Good for the Poor Miserable SLAVES. Guaranteed! End of Footnote.}

Can you walk into the US Capitol? ∧

Visitors are welcome to enter the building **through** the **Capitol** Visitor Center, located underground on the east side of the **Capitol. You can** begin your **Capitol** experience at the Visitor Center by visiting our temporary exhibits, perusing our Gift Shops or dining in our Restaurant.

www.visitthecapitol.gov › plan-visit
Plan A Visit | U.S. Capitol Visitor Center

The United States **Capitol** in Washington, **D.C.**, is a symbol of the American people and their government, the meeting place of the nation's legislature.

How far apart are the White House and the Capitol?

2 miles

The distance between White House and Capitol Hill is **2 miles**. Jun 29, 2020

www.rome2rio.com › White-House › Capitol-Hill-DC-USA
White House to Capitol Hill - 6 ways to travel via line 32 bus, and

Does the President actually live in the White House? ∧

The **White House** is the official residence and workplace of the **president** of the United States. It is located at 1600 Pennsylvania Avenue NW in Washington, D.C., and has been the residence of every U.S. **president** since John Adams in 1800.

en.wikipedia.org › wiki › White_House
White House - Wikipedia

08-02B |_| However, if the Concrete is made with Fresh Cement, Volcanic Ash, and NO Added Chemical Poisons to Ruin it, such Concrete should Endure for 10,000 Years, or more, if it is Protected from the Weather by Ceramic Tiles, and a Roof. Notice the Heavy Concrete Foundation Blocks that we made for the Concrete Columns or Pillars to Rest on, which are 2-feet square and 9 feet Tall. There are 35 of those in the House, which Support the Solid Concrete Walls, which are 8-inches Thick and 9 feet Tall, which Support the Concrete Roof, which should have been made in Concrete STEPS, for each Room, without any Rusty Steel Reinforcement Bars, and "Welded Together" with one large Concrete Slab that Covers the entire Roof, which would "Lock" all of the Steps Together, and provide a Strong Flat Floor for the next Story going Up; but, we were too Poor to Do it Riit: beCause of being Victims of Capitalism, which can never Afford to Do anything Correctly, whose Capitol Dome had to be "Fixed," or "Repaired," not long ago, at a Cost of more than 56 Times the Original Dome: beCause of that Evil Thing called INFLATION, which is just another Edomite Invention and Trick of the Devil to Devalue the Dollar, and make Endless Slaves of the Masses of Ignorant People, who are not Aware of the Fact that a Pair of Shoes Costed the same Amount at the Time of Jesus Christ, as they did at the Time of Father Abraham, about 2,000 Years earlier: beCause, there was NO Inflation! Also, Notice that all Good Buildings were Built Centuries, or even thousands of Years Ago — such as the Parthenon in Greece, and the Pantheon in Rome, which has a Concrete Domed Roof, which should be there for another 10,000 Years, if American Air Force "Heroes" do not Drop a Smart Bomb into the Oculus, and Destroy that Ancient Work of the SAINTS, who are Righteous People, who Do their Best to Do Things Correctly, who do not give a Damn about PROFITS: beCause, that is the Least of their Concerns: beCause, they are not Attempting to take Advantage of Poor Ignorant SLAVES; but, they are Trying to Do what is RIIT. Therefore, they are the Good People, who will Inherit the Holy Kingdom of All that is GOOD, which is GOD, who Loves Good People and Good Governments. †§‡§§

08-03 [_] O Holy Moses, why are you so Angry? Why are you Swearing? Can you not Write your Book without getting ANGRY at Ignorant Politicians, Preachers, and School Teachers, who cannot be Rightly Blamed for not Teaching TRUTHS that they were never Tawt? Indeed, they are as Innocent as little Newly-born Lambs, who have no Idea what *Good Government* is all about: beCause, the so-called *"Holy Bible"* never Mentions it! In Fact, anyone can get on the Internet, and Search for the *Blue Letter Bible,* and Discover more than 12 Different Translations to Choose from, and Search for *Good Government,* and this is all that they will get, to Piss them Off: †§‡§§

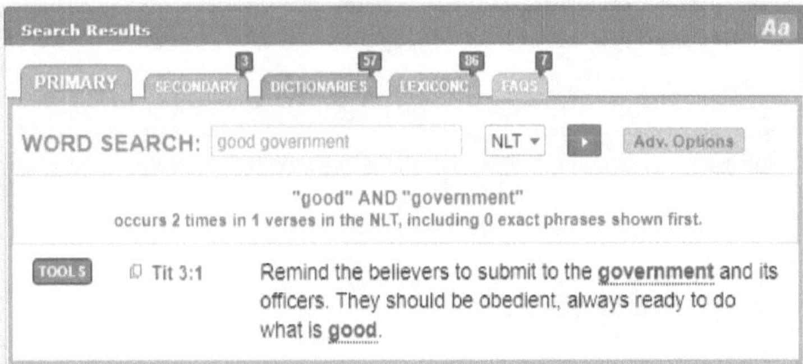

08-04 [_] Well, my Friend, the NLT stands for *New Living Translation,* which seems to be just as Dead as the other Translations: beCause, that is how Satan Wanted it: beCause he Loves Slavery, and Hopes to God that it goes on forever and ever: beCause, he is Seeking to Destroy ALL of Mankind: beCause he Envies God and his Saints, who are People who Seek to Say and Do what is RIIT, which is GOUD, even if it seems to be Speld WRong: beCause, it is Spelled according to some Consistent Reliable RULES, according to the Swanky FUNETIK Ingglish KEE TQ PROONUNSEEAASHUN, which has one Way to spell one Sound, instead of 5, 10, 20 or 100 Ways, as in the Case of "OO" in School, fool, rule, do, two, shoe, crew, blue, through, Sioux, lieu, maneuver, rhubarb, rheumatism, rendezvous, prosciutto, group, ghoul, and pooh, which koud all be speld with a Q — like this: Skql, fql, rql, dq, 2, shq, krq, blq, thrq, Sq, lq, munqver, rqbrrb, rqmutizm, rondaavq, prooshqtoo, grqp, gql, and pq; but, that would be far too easy for the School Children to LERN, who might even say: "Tq Hel with gooing tq School: beeKawz, ii kan Reed and Riit mii oon Werdz, and spel Knowledge az N-O-L-I-J, instead of K-N-O-W-L-E-D-G-E, which is much more Accurate than Fake knowledge: beCause Nolij is Correct, while Stupidity is NOT Correct, and Insanity is for Satan and Sons, Incorporated, who can all go Straat to HEL!"

When mama **cows** were separated from their babies, they made a higher pitched, louder call. ... The calves themselves gave a distinct **moo** when they wanted milk but couldn't find their mothers. **Cattle** geneticist Jared Decker grew up on a farm in New Mexico. He says **cows** often **moo** to communicate with each other. May 16, 2016

www.harvestpublicmedia.org › post › why-do-cows-m... ▾
Why Do Cows Moo? Here Are A Few Reasons | Harvest ...

Cows vocalize for a number of reasons and usually if they are **mooing** it's because they are unhappy. A group of happy **cows** is usually silent other than the munching sound they make while chewing cud or eating. ... Another call is that of a **cow** looking for herdmates.

www.quora.com › Why-do-cows-moo
Why do cows moo? - Quora

Some **cows** will also **moo** when they are looking to find a mate. Finding other **cows** in **the** herd is part of why these animals **moo**, but there are other reasons, **too**. In **the** wild, **cows** are prey animals. Sometimes **mooing** attracts predators, but sometimes **cows** can also use their moos to help keep each other safe. Feb 21, 2018

askdruniverse.wsu.edu › 2018/02/21 › why-do-cows-moo

Why do cows moo? | Ask Dr. Universe | Washington State University

If you ask a child what noises **cattle make** he will say "Moo." **Cattle** can **make** several different **sounds** including mooing, bellowing, snorting and grunting, and they use these noises for different things. People who spend a lot of time with **cattle** can tell what sort of mood the herd is in by the noises they are **making**.

animals.mom.me › noises-cattle-make-6436

What Noises Do Cattle Make? | Animals - mom.me

These moos are the pick-up lines of the **cattle** world. Bulls and **cows** let each other know that they are ready to, in the words of a bovine Marvin Gaye, get it on. They've lost their calf or their mom. ... The calves themselves gave a distinct **moo** when they wanted milk but couldn't find their mothers. May 16, 2016

www.harvestpublicmedia.org › post › why-do-cows moo-...

Why Do Cows Moo? Here Are A Few Reasons | Harvest Public Media

How far away can you hear a cow moo?   ⌃

5 miles

You can guess the age of a **cow** that has horns by counting the number of rings on the horns. **Cows** have almost total 360 degree panoramic vision and are able to see colors, except red. **They can** detect odors up to 5 miles **away**. **Cows can hear** lower and higher frequencies better than humans.

www.veganpeace.com › animal_facts › Cows

Animal Facts - Cows - Vegan Peace

Cows moo at **night** to communicate to the rest of the herd and, often, to protect them from some kind of danger that is lurking in the shadows.

farmhouseguide.com › why-do-cows-moo-at-night

Why Do Cows Moo At Night? | Farmhouse Guide

{**FOOTNOTE 06.** So, when you Hear your Cows Mooing at Night, it is Best to Check on them, and see what is Threatening them, who might have just Woke Up from having a Nightmare with Horses Chasing after them, and running them over Cliffs. After all, Cows do Dream.}

Do cows bond with humans?

"We still form **bonds** with these animals, especially ones we work with closely," says Swanson. "Farmers may form a **bond** with the lead **cow**, or a veterinarian might **bond** with an animal who had a difficult birth and required special care." Dec 12, 2018

cvm.msu.edu › news › perspectives-fall-2018 › the-bond-...
The Bond between Humans and Livestock | College of Veterinary ...

Conclusion: Yes, **Cow do cry** when they are in painful condition. As far as flowing out of tears are concerned, they may flow when eyes get dry in summer or some sort of irritation or problem, so when you see tears doesn't mean they are **crying!** Animals **do** feel like human...

www.quora.com › Do-cows-cry
Do cows cry? - Quora

How do you know when a cow is happy?

Positive behavioural signs we look for in cows to know that they are feeling well include:

1. Cud chewing and rumination (check out this video to learn more)
2. Walking freely.
3. Interacting socially.
4. Grazing and eating well.
5. Bright eyes, clean and shiny coat and wet shiny nose.

   More items... • Aug 22, 2019

www.dairy.com.au › dairy-matters › you-ask-we-answer
How do you know if a cow is happy? - Dairy Australia

Here are some of the **reasons cows moo**: They are trying to find their friends. When **cows** change environments, like moving from one farm to another, they will **moo** to try to connect with their friends as they figure out their new surroundings. May 16, 2016

www.harvestpublicmedia.org › post › why-do-cows-moo-...
Why Do Cows Moo? Here Are A Few Reasons | Harvest Public Media

If they are cranky they will swish their tail from side to side, they will also dig up dirt with their front feet, they will hold their head up and stare at **you** and sometime snort **if you** get to close. Watch their ears as well as **cattle** are very sensitive to sound so these are a good sign.

www.farmstyle.com.au › news › understanding-cattle-beh...
Understanding Cattle Behaviour on Small Farms | Farmstyle Australia

According to research, **cows** are generally quite **intelligent** animals who can remember things for a long time. Animal behaviorists have found that they interact in socially complex ways, developing friendships over time and sometimes holding grudges against other **cows** who treat them badly. May 5, 2020

www.peta.org › animals-used-for-food › factory-farming

The Hidden Lives of Cows | PETA

Cows have incredible memories and can easily remember an **recognize** individual faces. Lots of sanctuaries have reported **cows** running over to greet visitors that they have not seen in over six months or longer.

www.onegreenplanet.org › little-known-things-cows-do

Wow! Did You Know Cows Did These 10 Things? - One Green ...

Cows can **show affection** by licking each other, it is often done by the animal lower in rank for an animal of higher rank within the herd. ... They will also lick their calves and they can form strong bonds of friendship with other **cows**.

www.quora.com › How-do-cows-show-affection-toward-...

How do cows show affection toward each other? - Quora

While **cows** may doze off for a few minutes at a time while standing up, they typically lie down to sleep or simply to rest, usually leaning forward on their chest and forelimbs or lying completely on their sides.

animals.mom.me › cow-sleep-standing-4379

Does a Cow Sleep Standing? | Animals - mom.me

Why **do cows** moo at **night**? - Quora. All the dairy **cows** in the dairy complex mooed so loudly at **night** that the entire town was kept awake. ... The mothers would cry all day and **night** for their lost babies, often for days.

www.quora.com › Why-do-cows-moo-at-night

Why do cows moo at night? - Quora

Cows Love Their Babies

The most powerful relationship for a **cow** is that between a mother and **baby**. ... The mother-child bond continues after weaning; mothers and **their** children remain close to each other for life. **There** is also a sense of maternal community as other **cows** in the herd will help nurture **calves** if necessary.

www.onegreenplanet.org › animalsandnature › things-to-l...

10 Things to Love About Cows - One Green PlanetOne Green Planet

08-05 |_| So, O Holy Moses, will we have to Change our Ways of Spelling Words, just to Please thee? Will we have to Adopt the Old Elizabethan English System, with all of the "thee's, thou's, thine's, wouldest's, couldest's, and shouldest's," just to OBEY the Government

Officials, as the Apostle Paul wrote in *Romans 13,* saying: *Let every Soul be in Submission to the Higher Powers: beCause there are no Powers in this World of Woes, which are not Ordained by Satan, the Devil, which you can easily Prove, at:* "The GREAT Worldwide TELEVISED Court HEARING!" (That Great Meeting of the Most-Intelligent and Well-Educated Minds!) By The Worldwide People's Revolution!® Book 041B: *beCause they all LOVE CONFUSION, Tax Money, etc., etc.: beCause they are Ordained by the Author of Confusion, who is SATAN!* — Mockingbird's Version, in Plain English? Indeed, only an IDIOT would Think that K-N-O-W-L-E-D-G-E is the Correct Way to spell NOLIJ; but, that is the Official Satanic Way of Doing it: beCause, it is Traditional to Spell Words like the Barbarians spell them, and we dare not Fix them, lest all of those Smart Children DROP OUT of "The Public School of IGNERUNT FQLZ!" (HOW we have been GRAATLEE DISEEVD by Capitalism!) By The Worldwide People's Revolution!® Book 024B, and take up Reeding the Inspired Books of the Colorful Peacock from Angel Ridge, at King's Mountain, Kentucky 40442 United States of Reason and Logic, which Rij Unwise People have Transformed into another American TRASH DUMP: beCause, if you do not get Caught by the one and only County Sheriff, you can Dump all of your Trash and Garbage into the Woods, in the Forest: beCause it is FREE, while the Public Trash Dump, or "Landfill," Costs 5$ for one Pickup Load. Therefore, why would anyone Waste Gas and Time to Drive to the Landfill, when they can just Drive into the Woods, and DUMP their Trash? Only an Ignorant FOOL would do otherwise in the Capitalist System: beCause, it is Designed to Produce CRIMINALS, which is very Profitable for Deceptive Lawyers, Unjust Judges, and Wicked Politicians, who should be Forced on a Chain Gang to Gather Up all of that Trash, whereby they might Decide to CHANGE their Laws and Rules, and Do what is RIIT! Yes, they would have to Adopt: "The CONSTITUTION for the New RIGHTEOUS One-World Government!" (HOW all Peoples can get True Justice, and Celebrate the Great Year of JUBILEE!) By The Worldwide People's Revolution!® Book 016B, which Requires Liberated People to Grow their own Foods in their own All-Mineral Organic Gardens, at HOME, where they all Belong, in their own Gardens of Eden, even as God Planned it from the Beginning, when he Created Adam and Eve in that Holy Garden, and told them that they were Free to Eat all of the Fruits and Nuts and Vegetables in the Garden, which they might have an Appetite for, which they did, until Mother Eve was Deceived by Satan, who Appeared to her as a Lying Innocent Colorful Snake, whom she did not Recognize as a BAD Creature to Keep Company with: beCause, she was just another Mindless Brainless FEMALE, who should not have been left alone with the Devil: beCause, she Needed the Wisdom of her Husband, who Knew for a Fact that the Tree, which Represented the Nolij of ALL that is Good and Evil, was a Dangerous Tree to be Eating from: beCause, it was Covered with THORNS, which were WARNING SIGNS that it was Forbidden Fruit, in spite of the Pretty Rainbow Colors, which made it the most Beautiful Tree in the entire Garden, Except for the Fruits on the Tree of LIFE, which were Exceedingly WHITE and Glowing with LOVE and Compassion, which were no Great Temptation to Eat; but, they were Pure and Satisfying, when Eaten with the Dark Green Leaves, which Supplied the Vitamins and Minerals: beCause they are for the Healing of the Nations, while the Sweet Fruits Supplied the Energy and Brain Power to THINK and Remember. But, of course, Mother Eve did not Spot that Tree of Life: beCause she was Lusting after … †‡§§

08-06 [_] So, my Friend, why did you not say what she was Lusting after? Was it Shameful? †§‡

08-07 [_] Well, O Holy Moses, she was Lusting after False Knowledge and Sensual Pleasures: beCause that Snake crawled into her Vagina, and Tickled her, which I did not Want to Reveal: beCause, some of the Old Ladies might be Offended by it; but, since you Asked me, I had to Answer your Question: beCause, it is Time for no more Hidden Secrets, which are most often Centered around SEX, even as any Horny Womb-man can Tell you, if she is Perfectly Honest. †§‡

Here are top 10 sign of a happy person.

1. They don't play the blame game. ...
2. They are kind and compassionate. ...
3. They have fewer expectations. ...
4. They don't think of themselves as victims. ...
5. They do not put others down. ...
6. They live in the present. ...
7. They are good at embracing changes. ...
8. They **know** how to express gratitude.

Nov 2, 2015

listsurge.com › top-10-signs-of-a-happy-person ▾

Top 10 Signs of a Happy Person | ListSurge

Ways to Tell If Someone Is Truly Happy

1. The first sign that you would notice **if someone** is truly **happy if** that **someone** starts to make long term plans. ...
2. Another good thing that would help you **tell if someone is happy** is if you find that person have a smile on his or her face all the time. ...
3. A person who is **happy** is definitely optimistic. ...
4. Get out of bed easily.

More items... • Feb 5, 2012

ezinearticles.com › Ways-to-Tell-If-Someone-Is-Truly-Ha...

Ways to Tell If Someone Is Truly Happy - Ezine Articles

There are three main things that **make people happy**: close relationships, a job or past-time that they love and helping others. On the other hand, money and material things do not have a lot to do with happiness, and **people** who emphasize them are less **happy** than those who do not.

study.com › academy › lesson › research-on-happiness-w...

Research on Happiness: What Makes People Happy? - Video ...

How can you tell if someone is happy in a picture?

In an authentic smile the eyelids drop, and the eyebrows lower accompanied by a symmetrical smile (see the **picture** on the right). Duchenne's research showed that the Zygomatic muscles that span the side of the face and attach to the corners of the mouth are also are attached to the Orbicularis Oculi. May 22, 2019

merrillresearch.com › how-can-you-tell-if-someone-is-trul...

How Can You Tell if Someone is Truly Happy? - Merrill Research

Who are the happiest people?

2019 report

Overall rank	Country or region	Healthy life expectancy
1	Finland	0.986
2	Denmark	0.996
3	Norway	1.028
4	Iceland	1.026

40 more rows

en.wikipedia.org › wiki › World_Happiness_Report

World Happiness Report - Wikipedia

Some physical signs of anger include:

1. clenching your jaws or grinding your teeth.
2. headache.
3. stomach ache.
4. increased and rapid heart rate.
5. sweating, especially your palms.
6. feeling hot in the neck/face.
7. shaking or trembling.
8. dizziness.

www.mentalhelp.net › anger › recognizing-signs

Recognizing Anger Signs - MentalHelp.net

Being of service to others not only helps them – **it makes you** feel **happy** that **you** could **make** a difference.

...

5 Things That Will Make You Happier Every Day

- Exercise more. ...
- Sleep more. ...
- Help others. ...
- Smile already. ...
- Be Grateful.

{**FOOTNOTE 07.** Since I am the Healthiest Happiest Person that I Know, I have to Consult myself about the Subject of Happiness, which Naturally Begins with a Relationship with All that is GOOD, which is God, who Loves all Provable Truths, including the Truth concerning what Makes People HAPPY, who must be Free of all Guilt, who must not be Hiding their Sins, who must be Perfectly Honest about all Things, including the Governmental Sins, which are Bound to make all of the People Unhappy, if those Sins Effect/Affect them, which they usually do: beCause it is all about MONEY, which is not Easy to come by, and especially if you are a Really Poor Person, who is Mentally Poor, Physically Poor, Spiritually Poor, Materially Poor, Financially Poor, and so Poor as to not even have a Good Garden to Eat from, which could make a Person Extra Unhappy, if the Rain should Stop, and there is no Water for the Garden. Therefore, the "Secret" to True Happiness, is to be Set Up Properly for LIVING, which Spells: Swanky Fortresses.}

Happiness and emotional fulfillment are within your grasp.

- Be with others who make you smile. Studies show that we are happiest when we are around those who are also happy. ...
- Hold on to your values. ...
- Accept the good. ...
- Imagine the best. ...
- Do things you love. ...
- Find purpose. ...
- Listen to your heart. ...
- Push yourself, not others.

More items...

www.psychologytoday.com › blog › emotional-fitness

10 Simple Ways to Find Happiness | Psychology Today

{**FOOTNOTE 08.** I have no Idea what a "… bad inner of attitude" might be. The Person who wrote it obviously did not Proof-read it very well, which would make him or her Unhappy to Discover that; but, Thank God, it can easily be Fixed by Computers. However, there are many Things in this World of Woes, which cannot easily be Fixed — such as Cleaning up the Oceans, which are now Full of Trash, you might say, even though there is lots of Space in the Oceans for Trillions upon Trillions of TONS of Capitalist Trash, which the Trash-producers do not Object to: beCause, they do not have to Liv with it. In Fact, most of them never See it: beCause the Airplanes Fly too High in the Sky to makc such Trash Visible from up there; but, God has Telescopic Eyeballs, you might say, and so does the Living Conscience of anyone who is still Alive with all of his or her Senses Working Correctly. Trust me, Humanity will not be Truly Happy, until we get ourselves Straightened Out, and in Line with God, who Asks us to SHARE the Good Earth with one another, and Forget about Profits and "Making Money," which only Governments and Bankers can Do, who have Printing Presses and Minting Machines. Perhaps the Author meant to say: There is no Real Beauty in a Person who has no Inner Beauty, Peace, nor Happiness, who has a Bad Attitude toward Provable Truths, which should be Proven at: "The GREAT Worldwide TELEVISED Court HEARING!" (That Great Meeting of the Most-Intelligent and Well-Educated Minds!) By The Worldwide People's Revolution!® Book 041B, where each Important Subject can be Addressed in a Civilized Manner with a Righteous Judge in Charge of the Court, who has his Wisest Counselors nearby with their Laptop Computers in front of them, who Listen Carefully, and give their Good Advice to the Judge, who should give to those Counselors Credit for any Wisdom that they might Reveal: beCause such a Righteous Judge is not Seeking all of the Glory for himself; but, for everyone who Proclaims Provable Truths: beCause Honor should be Given to whomever is Honorable, and Ignorant Fools should Learn to Keep their Mouths SHUT, and Listen Intently to the HEARING. [_] Amen.}

08-08 [_] Well, I figured that it must have been something to do with Sex; but, I did not know that a Snake could Crawl into any Woman's

Vagina; but, I suppose that he could have been Licking on her, and Tickling her Clitoris, which would be very Sensual, which no one would Want to be Published in any Holy Bibles: beCause the little Girls and Boys might be Reeding it, and might even Discover that it was Represented by the Tree of the Nolij of All that is GOOD and EVIL! Yes, Satan was far more Subtle than most Ignorant People can Imagine: beCause, he Managed to get BILLIONS of People to Eat the Forbidden Fruit, which Caused them to Die a Spiritual Death: beCause of Learning the Difference between GOOD and EVIL. For Example, almost everyone Knows for a FACT that those Stinking Noisy Polluting DANGEROUS Automobiles are BAD for People; but, they go on Using them, anyway: beCause they have Hauled themselves to Work, and Hauled their Groceries Home: beCause, none of them have any Luscious All-Mineral Organic Gardens to Eat from: beCause, they never Heard of "The LUSCIOUS All-Mineral Organic Method of Gardening!" (HOW to Grow DELICIOUS Satisfying Foods for Potential Kingz and Kweenz in Beautiful Swanky PALACES!) By The Worldwide People's Revolution!® Book 021B, which is a Companion Book of: "Orgimmick Gardening at its Best!" (HOW to Grow Delicious Satisfying Foods without a 10 Million-Dollar Investment!) By The Worldwide People's Revolution!® Book 079, which are never Mentioned in "The Public School of IGNERUNT FQLZ!" beCause that would not be Profitable for the Education Slave Masters, who Gain BILLIONS of Dollars by "educating" the Ignorant Children with FALSE education, which does not even Capitalize Fake Knowledge, which can never Liberate the Education Slaves: beCause, they are Trapped in an EVIL Edomite Slavery System, which is not Willing to Confess that there are any "Guaranteed Solutions!" (HOW to Solve our Local and Global Problems in the Most-Rational Manner Possible!) By The Worldwide People's Revolution!® Book 080, for anything: beCause, those Solutions might put some (all) Lying Edomites Out of Business. †§‡

{FOOTNOTE 09. Jesus said something to the Effect that Sinners do not Want to come into the Light of Truths, lest their Evil Deeds should be Exposed, in *John 3*. *"And this is the Condemnation, that Light has come into the World; but, Evil Men Love the Darkness of Ignorance, more than the Bright Shining Light of Provable Truths: beCause their Deeds are Evil. Indeed, everyone who does Evil, Hates the Light of Truths, and will not come into the Light, lest his Evil Deeds should be Reproved; but, he who Practices Truths is Happy to come into the Light of a Courtroom: so that his Deeds might be made Known, that they are Worked according to the Will of God, who is All that is GOOD."* — NMV of Verse 19—21.

Therefore, all of the Righteous People will say a Hearty [_] AMEN!, and Check both Boxes with large Green-X Marks: beCause, they Agree! In Fact, how could they Disagree? WHY would they Disagree? If they do Disagree, it is Proof that they are Sinners of the Worst Kind, who have Secret Sins, which they do not Want to be Exposed. Otherwise, they would be Happy to come to Court, and Show to us that they are not Spiritual Cowards; but, Real Men of Strong Religious and Political Convictions, who are not Ashamed. ‡}

{Why would any of those People be Ashamed to come into a Courtroom? They are all Happy and Contented with Food and Fur, you might say! There were Times when they Practiced Segregation, and Separated themselves by their Colors; but, I would not know WHY.}

08-09 [_] For Example, there is a Picture of some "Profitable Swanky MULCHING ROCKS!" (30 Advantages for Using Swanky Mulching Rocks in an All-Mineral Organic Garden!) By The Worldwide People's Revolution!® Book 098, which can be Used Wisely in an Organic Garden, to make it Weedless, which Saves a lot of Time and Energy Hoeing Weeds, and also Holds in a LOT of Moisture, which will Save TRILLIONS upon TRILLIONS of Gallons of WATER, if we Use those Mulching Rocks Properly in Deserts, whereby the Gardens are Watered by Underground Ceramic Pipes, even as I have Explained in my Inspired Book, which can easily be Proven to be GOOD, at: "The GREAT Worldwide TELEVISED Court HEARING!" (That Great Meeting of the Most-Intelligent and Well-Educated Minds!) By The Worldwide People's Revolution!® Book 041B, which "The Swanky Associations of Working Soldiers!" (A Fascinating Collection of Various Kinds of Voluntary Working Soldiers!) By The Worldwide People's Revolution!® Book 018B, will be Happy to Learn about: beCause, they do not particularly Like to Waste a lot of Time nor Energy, HOEING WEEDS, when they can Employ some Mechanical Robots to Place those Mulching Rocks in their Exact Places in their All-Mineral Organic Gardens, for FREE! After all, those Robots will not Cost nearly as much as one of those Stinking Noisy Polluting DANGEROUS Cars: beCause, the Robot can Work all by itself! †§‡§§

08-10 [_] O Moses, I just LOVE my Pretty Red Car, in spite of all of the Pollution, Noise, and Dangers: beCause it Transports my Fat Ass all around Town, which would not be the Case within those "**GLORIOUS Swanky Hotels Castles and Fortresses!**" which use Elevators, Escalators and Electric Subway Trains for Transportation. Indeed, I Worship my Car, and cannot Wait to Buy the Latest Model of an ELECTRIC Car, in spite of the Fact that the Great Grandchildren will have NO LITHIUM for making Batteries to Power their Laptop Computers, if we Capitalist Fools Waste all of that Lithium in our New Cars: beCause, like Motor Oil and Gasoline, the Earth has a Limited Amount of it, which God Intended would last for no less than 20 Million Years, if we just Used it WISELY, and did not Waste it on any Selfishness, Greed, PRIDE, nor whatever it is that makes us INSANE, who Vainly Imagine that the Great Grandchildren will Love us for Wasting it, when they should HATE us for it, and even dig up our Graves, and BURN our Bones in Nazi Ovens, just for Kissing the Asses of those Lying Conniving Edomites, who Know the Truth of it. †§‡§§

— Chapter 09 —

Will the Masses of People Humbly Submit to Provable Truths?

09-01 [_] First of all, they must be Confronted with those Provable Truths, before they can Decide what is Best for them: beCause, as of now, they have no Idea what is Good for them, being like little Babies, who are Unaware that there are no less than 5,000 Varieties of Mangos to Choose from, for Example, as well as 5,000 Different Kinds of Apples, which they have never Tasted. Therefore, how can they Judge what they should Want? How can they make up their Minds about anything? Would any Civilized Father Invite a Police Officer to come into his House to Guard him from his own Children, who might Sneak into his Bedroom at Night, and Stab him in the Back with a Butcher Knife, just beCause those Children did not get to Watch some Cartoon on TV? No.

09-02 [_] O Moses, you Discovered the True Nature of People, when you brought the Children of Israel out of Egypt, who were Lusting after the Flesh Pots of Egypt: beCause, all of those Spicy Meats Taste a lot Better than those Insipid Fruits, most of which are not Fit to Eat: beCause they were not Grown by "The LUSCIOUS All-Mineral Organic Method of Gardening!" (HOW to Grow DELICIOUS Satisfying Foods for Potential Kingz and Kweenz in Beautiful Swanky PALACES!) By The Worldwide People's Revolution!® Book 021B. However, if you Conducted a Scientific Experiment, and got 100 People Really HUNGRY, and then Fed some Truly GOOD Sweet Juicy Fruits to them, like those Mangos that are Pictured above Verse 03-03, I dare say that at least 90% of them would Agree that those Mangos are Far Superior to any Dog Foods or Hog Slop that might be for Sale at the Death and Hell Restaurant. However, without Really GOOD Fruits, you could not Persuade them to Accept the Garden-of-Eden Diet: beCause there are no Good Fruits to Eat. Therefore, in Order to Persuade the Masses of People to Accept that Garden-of-Eden Plan, what the World most Desperately Needs is at least ONE Good Example.

09-03 [_] Well, my Friend, if you had some Way to Communicate with the Masses of People at the same Time, and ALL of the People, you might Discover 10,000 or so, who might be Interested in being Scientific about it, and Willing to Experiment with a Garden-of-Eden Diet — except that it would Require 5 to 10 Years, just to get some Good Fruits on their Tables: beCause Fruit Trees do not Produce like Rats, Rabbits, nor Chickens: beCause, they Require TIME, just to Grow Up!‡

09-04 [_] O Moses, those 10,000 Volunteers would have to have "The Seven Basic Spiritual Building Blocks of LIFE!" (Faith Hope Trust Love Patience Persistence and Obedience!) By The Worldwide People's Revolution!® Book 036, just to Endure such a Test, and you would have to be in Charge of them, Personally: beCause, no one else would Qualify to Govern them! Therefore, it is now a Worse Situation, than it was when you brought the Children of Israel Out of Egypt: beCause Satan's Servants have many more Temptations than they used to have, and Countless Eating Pits to Fall Headlong Into! In Fact, the Air is Full of the Odors of Cooked Foods, whereby a Person could hardly Escape from the Temptations, unless he went into the Wilderness of Peace, where there are Zero Temptations: beCause there is nothing there to EAT, and probably nothing to Drink: beCause, even the Water is Polluted with Acid Rains, which makes it Unfit to Drink. Therefore, the Masses of People are not going to go along with the Swanky Fortress Plan: beCause they cannot Visualize that Lifestyle being Superior to their Present Lifestyle, even if it is a Hell on Earth: beCause, it is like Trading your Wife for one that you have never Seen. Therefore, it will Require "The New RIGHTEOUS One-World Government!" (HOW to Establish a Righteous One-World Government without Going to

WAR!) By The Worldwide People's Revolution!® Book 056, just to Build those "GLORIOUS Swanky Hotels Castles and Fortresses!" (Beautiful Planned City States for WISE Intelligent Well-Educated People with Common Sense and Good Understanding!) By The Worldwide People's Revolution!® Book 019B, whereby we might Obtain even ONE Good Example for the People to SEE, and to Lust after it: beCause, without something Good to Lust after, no one is going to get very Interested. †§‡

09-05 |_| Well, my Friend, no matter how many Times that you Roll it Around within the Belly of your Mind, it always comes right back Around to the Fact that we Tax Slaves must DEMAND: "The GREAT Worldwide TELEVISED Court HEARING!" (That Great Meeting of the Most-Intelligent and Well-Educated Minds!) By The Worldwide People's Revolution!® Book 041B, just to Discover how many People might be Interested in Liberty and Justice for ALL.

09-06 [_] O Moses, "The New RIGHTEOUS One-World Government!" will not be any Better than the Elected Officials, who will have to be Real Leaders, just to get anyone to Follow them. Therefore, HOW are you going to Discover the Best of Men to Govern that Good Government? ‡

09-07 |_| Well, my Friend, it is for Sure that I am not going to Discover them, while sitting all alone in my House, Hoping that the Masses of People will somehow Discover what I Teach, while Watching their Televisions, which never Mention anything that I Teach. Moreover, it is not like anyone is Searching on the Internet, for: "Good Lessons for Honest Wise Men!" (A Simplistic Plan for Totally Solving the Complicated Problems of Deceived Mankind!) By The Smarter Professor of Common Sense! Book 125, much less, for: "The Sixth Book of Moses called GOOD GOVERNMENT!" (The Primary Missing Book in the Holy Bible!) By The Worldwide People's Revolution!® Book 126. Therefore, someone would have to Spend a LOT of Money to ADVERTISE all such Books, which I do not have — do YOU? Of course NOT! So, our Hands are TIED, you might say: beCause we are Limited by a Lack of MONEY. However, it is no Secret that Politicians can Raise MILLIONS of Dollars for their Election Deception Campaigns: beCause they are usually Promising Government Assistance, if they get Elected, while I am Tormenting their Souls by Proposing that they should Join: "Seven Great Armies of Working Soldiers!" (HOW to Provide a Way for Everyone to WORK: so as to Eliminate Poverty, Crimes, Drug Abuses, Prisons and

Unnecessary Taxes!) By The Worldwide People's Revolution!® Book 015B, which Sounds like going to WAR to an Idiot, who never Stops to THINK about the Beauty of WORKING Soldiers, who are making War on those hundreds of thousands of Mountains of Rocks, which do not Object to it: beCause they were Created to be Used WISELY. However, the Sluggard would say that those Mountains should not be TOUCHED!

09-08 [_] Yes, O Moses, those Mountains are SACRED, and should not be Touched: beCause, like it or not, the Trees are RENEWABLE, while the Rocks are NOT. Therefore, we should continue to Build our Wooden / Plastic Firetrap Mouse-infested Cockroach Dens, which have Eternal Heating and Cooling Bills, Insurance Payments, Interest Slavery, and all of those Good Things, which you HATE; but, I Love them: beCause, I am an Insurance Agent, whose Favorite Brother is a Rich Squirrelly Banker, who Collects Millions of Dollars from Interest and Mortgage Payments: beCause, he is doing a Necessary Service for Mankind, which you do not Appreciate: beCause, you do not Want to Play the Edomite Money Game, called Capitalism; but, I LOVE it, and so does my Favorite Brother, whose Cousin is the County Tax Assessor, who uses Good Judgment, and makes Sure that those Unwanted "Niggers" have to Pay Extra Property Taxes, whereby they are Forced to MOVE OUT, who just Naturally Move into some Poor Niggerville on the South Side of the Railroad Tracks, where other Poor Negros Liv, who have no Idea HOW they are going to Escape from their Miserable State of Extreme Poverty: beCause, they are TRAPPED! †§‡§§

09-09 [_] Well, O Insurance Agent, you are Seeking to Justify Wickedness, which makes you Eligible for some other Capitalists to Repay you a Hundredfold, which will Please the God of Justice, who Knows that you Deserve all of your Sicknesses, Diseases, Accidents, Debts, Worries, Fears, and whatever you Suffer with: beCause, you are not Worthy of True Freedom, nor Liberty.

09-10 [_] So, O Moses, are you Suggesting that Mankind must go on Suffering for another thousand Years, or more, just to Wake Up and come to their Riit Senses? Does that seem to be True Justice, to you? What about the Goodness of Capitalism, which has Lifted more People Out of Poverty than any other Economic System? For Example, the Chinese People used to be Extremely Poor; but, now they have become Moderately RICH, whereby 99% of them get to Liv in Tiny Apartments, where there is barely enough Space to Turn Around, and no Gardens, at all, who used to Liv on little Farms, and had Room to Breathe; but, now the Air is so Thick with Pollution, that a Person can hardly Breathe, which is True Progress — Thanks to Capitalism, which is the Economic Salvation of Mankind, which was Tawt by the First Church of Jesus Christ, in *the Book of Acts,* which Reveals that Saint Peter Collected all of the Money for himself, and put it into Jewish Banks, whereby he Collected Interest on it, and made himself so Rich that he Built Saint Peter's Basilica, in Rome, which is still Standing there to See in all of its Beautiful Naked Glory! †§‡§§

— Chapter 10 —

Civil Rights

10-01 [_] So, O Moses, what are Civil Rights? And how come you never Mentioned them in the Holy Bible? Were you Afraid of Democracy, during those Days? Could People not even "VOTE for The GOAT!" (The New Political Party that has Guaranteed Solutions for our Massive Problems!) By The Worldwide People's Revolution!® Book 109. Were they all SLAVES? †§‡

Civil rights are an essential component of democracy. They're guarantees of equal social opportunities and protection under the law, regardless of race, religion, or other characteristics. Examples are the rights to vote, to a fair trial, to government services, and to a public education. In contrast to civil liberties, which are freedoms secured by placing restraints on government, civil rights are secured by positive government action, often in the form of legislation.

Unlike human rights or natural rights, in which people acquire rights inherently—perhaps from nature—civil rights must be given and guaranteed by the power of the state. Therefore, they vary greatly over time, culture, and form of government and tend to follow societal trends that condone or abhor types of discrimination. For example, the civil rights of the LGBTQ community have only recently come to the forefront of political debate in some democracies.

When the enforcement of civil rights is found by many to be inadequate, a civil rights movement may emerge in order to call for equal application of the laws without discrimination.

The marginalization of African Americans spurred the American civil rights movement, beginning in the 1950s and growing throughout the early 1960s. That movement, based mainly in African American churches and colleges of the South, involved marches, boycotts, and civil disobedience, such as sit-ins. Most efforts were local, but the impact was felt at the national level—a model of civil rights organizing that has since spread all over the globe.

Civil rights include the ensuring of peoples' physical and mental integrity, life, and safety; protection from discrimination on grounds such as race, gender, sexual orientation, gender identity, national origin, color, age, political affiliation, ethnicity, religion, and disability; and individual **rights** such as ...

Though the scope of the term differs between countries, civil liberties may include the freedom of conscience, freedom of press, **freedom of religion**, freedom of expression, **freedom of assembly**, the right to security and liberty, freedom of speech, the right to privacy, the right to equal treatment under the law and due ...

They guarantee **rights** such as religious freedom, freedom of the press, and trial by jury to all **American citizens**. First Amendment: Freedom of religion, freedom of speech and the press, the right to assemble, the right to petition government.

In the 1860s, Americans adapted this usage to newly freed blacks. Congress enacted **civil rights** acts in 1866, 1871, 1875, 1957, 1960, 1964, 1968, and 1991.

10-02 [_] Now, as you can See, Congress Changed their Rules about Civil Rights, several Times: beCause, the Constitution was not quite Clear about all such Things: beCause the *Holy Bible* was not Clearly Understood: beCause the Authors did not Foresee the Problems that would Arise during the Future: beCause, at that Time in World History, the People had no such Problems: beCause, almost all of the People Lived in Houses with their Gardens nearby, which Occupied their Time and Energy, just to Feed and Clothe themselves. For Example, it Required a half-acre of Grapes, just for making Wine for a large Family. But then, as Civilization Grew, People began to fill up their Gardens and Orchards with Houses: beCause, Land became Expensive. Moreover, they also began to Educate themselves, and Wrote many Books, hundreds of Years before Christ. For Example, the Library of Alexandria had some 300,000 Books in it, which Library was Established by Alexander the Great, who was a Famous Greek General and War Lord, who never Lost a single Battle, who Conquered the known Civilized World, along with his Gay Lover, Hephaestion, who Grew Up Together. So, when Hephaestion suddenly Died from a Disease, his Death nearly Killed Alexander with Grief, which soon brought about his own Death with some Disease: beCause the Grief Greatly Weakened his Mind and Body, and Destroyed his Happiness: beCause he Loved Hephaestion so much, who was Closer to him than his own Wife. In Fact, it was a Love Affair that Resembled that of Jonathan and David, of whom David wrote: *"I am Greatly Distressed for you, my Brother Jonathan: because you have been very Pleasant to me, ever since I got to Know you. In Fact, your Love for me was Wonderful, surpassing the Love of any Womb-man, and I have had several of them; but, none of them Loved me as you have Loved me, with a Pure and True Love, even as all People should Love God for his Goodness and Beauty." — The Book of the Acts of King Solomon, First and Last.* Yes, Solomon also had his Lover, who could not Resist making his Confessions in his own Book, which the Lying Edomites Deleted. †§‡

10-03 [_] O Moses, did you not also Love Joshua with the same True Love? Were you not like True Brothers in Christ, who also Loved Saint John, even as David Loved Jonathan? In Fact, were they not both Reincarnated Spirits? I Mean, was John not Jonathan, and Jesus David, when they were Born Again as John and Jesus? Does that not make Perfect Sense to you, O Moses? In Fact, I would say that you and Joshua were Enoch and Jesus, himself, whose Spirit was being Perfected.

10-04 [_] Well, my Friend, all such Things are Mysteries to Mankind: beCause, Jehovah God did not Explain such Things to me, nor even to Enoch, as far as I Know; but, he did Reveal some of it to our Selected King, who is the Man with the Spirit of Elijah, whom *Malachi* wrote about; but, only with very few Words: beCause, it was not Safe to Reveal too much, whereby his little Book would not have been put into the *Holy Bible:* beCause, those Lying Conniving Edomites did not Believe in Reincarnation, in spite of it being Self-evident that all People are Reincarnated: beCause there is no other Way for God to get their Spirits Perfected for All that is Good: beCause, it Requires a lot of Experiences, just to Grow Up in Grace and in True Nolij. Therefore, we just have to be Patient, and Hope that we Learn as many Good Lessons during this Life, as Possible, and get those Lessons Embedded in our Souls, whereby we can Progress during the Next Life: beCause, there is Bound to be a Next Life, even if we must be Born in a New World, in some other Solar System, which is under the Administration of some other God: beCause, not all of the Gods are just Alike. In Fact, not even 2 of them are just Exactly Alike: beCause, they were also once upon a Time MEN, just like us, who were Born Again and AGAIN, until they were brought to Perfection in the Kingdom of the Most-High God, who only Requires that we Do our Best to get ourselves Perfected for All that is GOOD: beCause, what else can he Expect of us? We all have our Limits.

10-05 [_] So, O Moses, when we Meet someone, and there is an Instant Connection between us, does that Mean that we used to Know each other in some Previous Life? Or, am I just Dreaming?

10-06 [_] Well, there is a Good Possibility that we get to Meet Old Friends, and, that God Arranges it: beCause he Likes to Play his Games with us, just to Discover the True Natures of our Spirits. In Fact, it could be that we Knew someone Centuries Ago, and the Connection is Deep within our Souls, which can be Seen in our Eyes, and even in the Eyes of someone who is Fighting against us in a Battle, who would rather throw Down their Weapons, than to Hurt us: beCause of being Old Friends; but, they Seldom Yield to the Holy Spirit: beCause of being under the Influence of Tyrants, who Demand that we Kill them: beCause, they are so-called "Enemies," who would Agree with us, if we just had Rational Conversations about the Disputes between us. For Example, who can Rightly Deny that God Blest us with Mountains of Rocks to Work with, and Plenty of them, which come in all Colors and Kinds, which we should Share with each other, as True Brothers and Sisters? After all, the False Ownership Doctrine is Contrary to the Teachings of Father Abraham, who told his Nephew Lot, that if he Chose a certain Piece of Land, that he could have it. Therefore, Lot Chose the Plain of Jordan: beCause it was Fertile with Deep Rich Topsoil, at that Time, which Sounds like a Jewish Myth, to me: beCause most of that Land around there is nothing but a Desert. However, Nature can Dramatically Change Things, depending on Volcanoes and Earthquakes. §‡

10-07 |_| So, O Holy Moses, were not all of those Bible Stories just Inventions of the Jews, in Order to Sell Books, which had to Sound Authentic, like True Stories; but, they were Actually just Myths, which the Edomites Enhanced for their own Ungodly Gain? Otherwise, they might have wrote about Civil Rights, the Evilness of Slavery, Gay Marriages, Abortions, and whatever is going on, nowadays: beCause, the Natures of People have really not Changed very much during thousands of Years. Indeed, if they were Truly Holy Prophets, they must have Known about us? ‡

10-08 |_| Well, how much do you Know about the People who will be Living 4,000 Years from now? Can you Foresee whatever they will be Doing? Well, maybe you cannot Foresee it; but, I can; and I Foresee that most of the People will Finally come to their Right Senses, and Decide to Build those **"GLORIOUS Swanky Hotels Castles and Fortresses!" (Beautiful Planned City States for WISE Intelligent Well-Educated People with Common Sense and Good Understanding!) By The Worldwide People's Revolution!®** Book 019B: beCause of all of the Good Reasons and Great Advantages for Doing it, whereby each Kind of People can be Separated from the other Kinds: beCause, as the Holy Prophet Daniel Revealed, Iron and Clay do not Mix Well, and neither do White People and Black People: beCause, they have Contrary Natures, which is to be Expected: beCause, the Black and Brown Peoples came from Different Worlds, who were brought here by the Giants, in their Great Spaceships, to be their Slaves and Servants: beCause that was their Way of Managing their Affairs, which Worked fairly Well for them: beCause those Servants did not know what else to Do, other than to Obey their Masters: beCause, the Giants were Far more Intellectual than any of us, who Built most of the Great Kingdoms on this Good Earth, including the Parthenon in Athens, and other Great Stone Structures in the Mediterranean Nations, which the Greeks were Ashamed to Confess: beCause they Wanted to take the Glory for it, even as the Lying Jews Wanted to take the Glory for the Great Stonework in the Land of Israel. †§‡§§

10-09 |_| O Moses, even you Married a Dark-skinned Woman, in spite of your Blond Hairs and Blue Eyes, which was Contrary to Nature; and therefore, to be Perfectly Honest about it, you Loved Joshua much more than Zipporah, who had Brown Eyes, which was no Perfect Match, by any Means, which you probably Regretted doing; but, what Choice did you have, seeing that you were not Living among your own People, called Levites, most of whom had Blond Hairs and Blue Eyes, even as the Giants had Blond Hairs and Blue Eyes, before they got themselves Mixed Up with Heathen Nations? Indeed, it is now Happening to the White Races of People in this World of Woes, who are being Overcome by the Darker Races, who just Naturally Envy the White Races for their Superior Intellectual Abilities, which do not make them Better in the Eyes of Jehovah God: beCause he Judges by whatever is in our Hearts and Minds, whereby a Black Man can be Superior to a White Man, if he is Perfectly Humble and Honest about all Things; but, I would say that you would find it Difficult to Discover such a Humble and Honest Black Man among such Proud People with Big Muscles and Long Tally Whackers, who most often Win the Races, and whatever does not Require very many Brains to Achieve: beCause, they are often Physically Superior to White Men: beCause of being Used to many Generations of Difficult Work, who Need some Jewish Blood in them to be Intellectually Superior to other Black Men, just to Succeed, which got into some of them, Centuries Ago, when King Solomon was having Sex with African Women. †§‡

10-10 |_| Well, my Friend, it was not a Happy Marriage, as you Suggested; but, it was a Way of getting some Sexual Relief, and some Flesh-to-Flesh Contact, which everyone Needs, just to be Mentally Stable, which is what makes Prisons so BAD, which no Righteous Government would have: beCause there is a much Better Way to Handle Criminals and Transgressors of that Kind. However, as for the Pollution of the White Races by the Black Races, that Problem is Totally Solved by the more-Righteous Souls being Born in Mount Zion, to White Womb-men, whereby the White Races will not Die Off, as you might Fear: beCause Jehovah God Knows HOW to Save them and Preserve them for Governing all of the Nations, during the Future, when he will also Discover Men with Honest Light-brown Eyes and Dark Hairs to be

Rulers in the Kingdom: beCause, he does not Object to Darker People having Positions in his Holy Kingdom, if they just Qualify for it: beCause, it is Possible for them to be Equally as Righteous as the White People. †‡

— Chapter 11 —

Does a Righteous Government Need Prisons?

11-01 |_| Well, first of all, we must Understand that "The New RIGHTEOUS One-World Government!" is not Associated with the Present Governments of this World, which have their own Special Problems to Deal with, which are of no Concern to the Righteous Government that I Propose, and which our Selected King Proposes, whereby each State must have a City State within it, if Possible, which is one of those "GLORIOUS Swanky Hotels Castles and Fortresses!" which have their own Good Governments, which do not all Agree concerning just HOW that they should be Managed, except that each one has an Elected King or Queen, who Enforces the Elected Laws and Flexible Rules that each City State VOTES for: beCause, it is Basically a Democratic System in that Respect, except that only Qualified People get to Vote, who have Filled Out and File: "The Complete SURVEYS of our VALUES!" (SURVEYS of Religious Spiritual Political Governmental Sexual Social Moral Economical Business Labor Habitual and Miscellaneous VALUES!) By The Worldwide People's Revolution!® Book 059, or at least a Minimum of "The Simplistic SURVEYS of our VALUES!" Book 059B, which will Qualify them, no matter what their Answers to the Questions might be: beCause, we will at least Know that they are not Total Idiots, nor Criminals: beCause, Criminals will just Naturally Choose to Liv within their Present Cities of Confusion, rather than Volunteer to be Members of: "The Swanky Associations of Working Soldiers!" (A Fascinating Collection of Various Kinds of Voluntary Working Soldiers!) By The Worldwide People's Revolution!® Book 018B, who have to Do a Minimum of an Average of 4 Hours of Common Skilled Labor per Workday, just to Live within their "Beautiful Swanky PALACES!" (A New Concept in Living Habits — Swanky Palaces for Poor People!) By The Worldwide People's Revolution!® Book 066: beCause, it Requires a certain Amount of Work just to Feed and Water People, as well as make their Uniforms, Costumes, Furniture, Appliances, Tools, and whatever they Want. However, if they do not Want any Computers, Televisions, Radios, Electric Stoves, Washing Machines, Refrigerators, nor even Sinks to Wash their Hands in, that is also Okay: beCause, they can Cheerfully Choose to Liv with other People of Like-mindedness. In Fact, they can Choose to Liv in "Beautiful Swanky Stone Dome Home

COMPLEXES!" (HOW to Build SECURE Tax-proof, Insurance-proof, Self-air-conditioned, Paint-proof, Rot-proof, Termite-proof, Mouse-proof, Fireproof, Tornado-proof, Hurricane-proof, Thief-proof, and BOMB-PROOF Houses!) By The Worldwide People's Revolution!® Book 102, in Groups of 20 or more People: beCause, they will be Plenty Spacious enough to Do that; but, no Fortress will be Permitted to make Tiny Cramped Houses to Liv in, which do not even have Storage Spaces for Trainloads of Capitalist TRASH, if they Want to Collect it; but, first of all, they will have to Explain WHY that they Want any such Vain Things: beCause, that seems to be just a bit Insane, I would say. In Fact, the next Photograph shows a little Painted Wooden House, which got itself Overcrowded with far too much of that Capitalist Trash; and therefore, those Black People had a Yard Sale, just to get some Freedom to Breathe, you might say, who were Glad to get Rid of it; but, hardly anyone Wanted to Buy it; and therefore, it sat there for Months, until they finally Gave it to the Salvation Army, which put it into some Warehouse, until they could make it Sellable for Pennies on the Dollar, whereby other Families Collected that Junk, most of which ended up in the Trash Dump: beCause, it was all just Trash, to begin with, which can easily be Proven in a Courtroom, which might have had some Use; but, not much. †§‡

11-02 [_] §§ The American Capitalists built hundreds of thousands of those Trash Dumps for the Black People: "… because that was all that they could afford," they said; "… and that one is in pretty good shape, when compared with some others." I was Informed that the Occupants did not really Care, and did not bother to do much Cleaning on the Inside of it: beCause, their Primary Interest was getting Drunk and Eating Barbecued Pork, which was their Idea of "Heaven on Earth."

11-03 [_] O Moses, what could anyone Expect from those Poor Abused Black People, who are generally Depressed by the Evil Ways that their Ancestors were Mistreated as SLAVES, who have never red: "HOW to Make Proper REPARATIONS!" (True Justice for Black and White People, and Everyone in Between them!) **By** The Worldwide People's Revolution!® Book 122

11-04 [_] Well, my Friend, I can Totally Relate with them: beCause, I had a Total of 12 Dollars to Play with, between the Ages of 6 and 14, which I Saved in my Piggy Bank, and then used that Money to Buy one of those Pretty Shiny German Pendulum Clocks, which I Gave to someone whom I Loved, for a Christmas Present, who did not even Thank me for it: beCause of being Ungrateful; or, beCause of Fearing that I might Love him too much, which he would not have known how to Handle: beCause he was as Straight as a Pin, and equally as Sharp and Dangerous. Actually, I now Believe that the Problem was the Old Rickety Wooden House that they Lived in, which Shook, or Vibrated when anyone Moved across the Floor, which Upset the Pendulum. †§‡

11-05 [_] So, O Moses, did you ever get him Converted to Jesus Christ? Did he ever become a Believer in Jesus? Was your Generosity not Rewarded in any Way? Or, was it a Total Loss? †§‡§§

11-06 [_] Well, my Friend, I have no Idea: beCause Jim Moved away, and I never saw that Family again; but, there is a Chance that he got "Converted" at some Billy Graham Crusade for Christ, who should reed: "Was Billy Graham Greatly Deceived?" (Giving Honor to whom Honor is Due!) By The Worldwide People's Revolution!® Book 083. After all, Great Crowds of People came to his HUGE Meetings, and got "Saved," they said; but, did they get Saved from their Sins?

{NOTE: The above Picture looks a lot Better in the 8.5 by 11-inch Colored Edition; but, you probably get the Point here. It is the Result of not having this Inspired Book in the *Holy Bible*. Most People Suffer for it, and will go right on Suffering, if we do not Do something about it.}

11-07 |_| Where are their Gardens? Where are their All-Mineral Organic Gardens? The entire City looks like a Capitalist Trash Dump, to me, and especially right down Town, where the Smog is the Thickest: beCause of the Old Unrepaired Cars, Buses and Trucks, which are Spewing Out Carbon Monoxide and Carbon Dioxide, which is what makes it such a Heavenly Place to Visit. Yes, it is "Home Sweet Home" to hundreds of thousands of Deceived People, who have no Idea what is Good for them. However, just a few Miles from there is a Wide-Open Space, where we could Build one of those **"GLORIOUS Swanky Hotels Castles and Fortresses!"** which would be an Inviting Place for them to Visit, who would most likely never Want to Return to the above Mess. Please be Perfectly Honest, and Check the above Box with a Green-X Mark, if you Agree. †§‡§§

11-08 [_] That is the closest thing that I can Discover on the Internet for "Beautiful Terraced Gardens." I am not sure that there is anything there to Eat; but, there might be some Berry Bushes. However, those little Terraces are nothing like the Grand Terraces within Swanky Fortresses, which would be at least 60 feet (18 meters) to 100 feet (30 meters) High, and 210 feet (64 meters) Wide, and Miles Long — depending on the Size of the Swanky Fortress, which might be 100 Miles in Diameter — which would be Planted with Various Kinds of Fruit Trees, Nut Trees, Berry Bushes, Grape Vines, Vegetable Gardens, and Flower Gardens, according to the Desires of **"The Swanky Association of Professional All-Mineral Organic Gardeners,"** who will have Artistic Designers, like the World has never Seen before: beCause, they will have an Unlimited Supply of Good Money to Work with, whereby they will be Free to Design anything that they Want to, if the other Working Soldiers are Willing to Do the WORK, which will not be Easy; but, it will be a LOT of FUN: beCause, it will be something that they WANT to Do, and without any Pay, except for getting to Eat at those "Royal Swanky Buffets!" (The Best Feasts in the Whole World!) By The Worldwide People's Revolution!® Book 103, and Living in those "Beautiful Swanky Stone Dome Home COMPLEXES!" which will Cost about 1 Billion Dollars, each, whereby no one can Complain about being Poor, anymore! And all of that is Possible, just by Obeying our Elected KING, who is only Asking for 4 Hours of Common Skilled Labor per Workday, on Average, from the MEN, only: beCause, all of the Wives will be Free to Stay at Home, or go Shopping at the FREE Swanky Grocery Stores, Shopping Mauls, or just Visit the Churches, Mosques, Synagogues, Temples, Golden Concert Halls, Cathedrals, Theaters, Gymnasiums, Tennis Courts, Heated Swimming Pools, Bowling Alleys, Roller Skating Rinks, Ice Skating Rinks, or whatever can be Found within those "Beautiful Swanky PALACES!" (A New Concept in Living Habits — Swanky Palaces for Poor People!) By The Worldwide People's Revolution!® Book 066, along with their Children and Husbands, whenever they get Off from Work, who will all be Healthy, Wealthy, and WISE, without any Money at all: beCause it is not Needed for True Prosperity, nor will any Riots, Protests, Sit-ins, Sit-downs, Sit-ups, nor Squat-benders be Needed: beCause, everyone will be getting Plenty of Exercise in their own Gardens, Vineyards, Orchards, and "Beautiful Swanky Stone Dome Home COMPLEXES!" (HOW to Build SECURE Tax-proof, Insurance-proof, Self-air-conditioned, Paint-proof, Rot-proof, Termite-proof, Mouse-proof, Fireproof, Tornado-proof, Hurricane-proof, Thief-proof, and BOMB-PROOF Houses!) By The Worldwide People's Revolution!® Book 102, which will have Home-craft Workshops and Sales Shops, just to make Life Interesting!

Yes, you may now take your Sweet Time to Produce some really GOOD Hand-crafted Furniture, if you Want to. †§‡

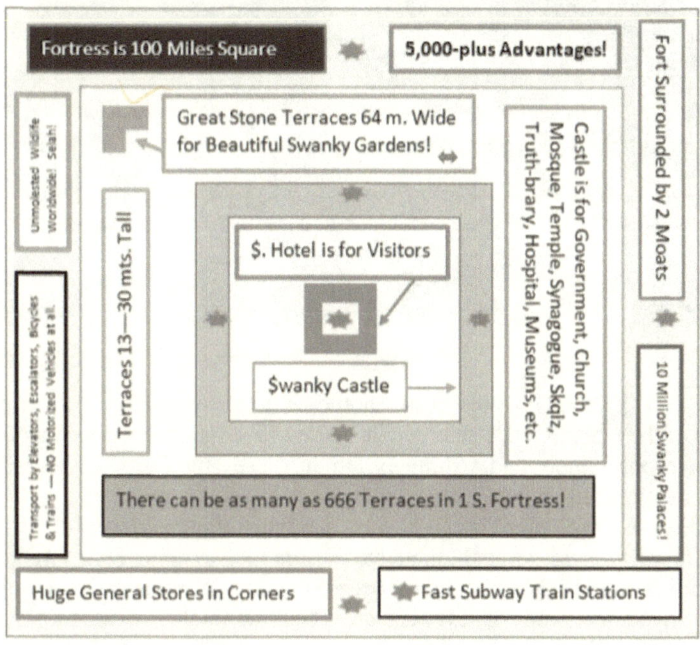

11-09 [_] ♦ So, O Moses, if we should Build those Swanky Fortresses, all of the Good Respectable People could Move into them, which would leave only Idiots and Criminals left in those Big Cities of Massive Confusion, who would soon get Converted to Jesus Christ: beCause they would be Constantly Praying to God that they might Survive, among all of the Criminals. After all, there would come a "Breaking Point" in their Hard Hearts: beCause of their Extreme Poverty, Worries, Fears, Deaths of Loved ones, and whatever Gangs of Outlaws might Provide for them: beCause, all of the Righteous People, and Intelligent People would simply MOVE OUT of those Hateful Cities of Confusion, with the Help of "The New RIGHTEOUS One-World Government!" and Move INTO those "GLORIOUS Swanky Hotels Castles and Fortresses!" (Beautiful Planned City States for WISE Intelligent Well-Educated People with Common Sense and Good Understanding!) By The Worldwide People's Revolution!® Book 019B, which would have NO Criminals in them: beCause, all of the Bad People would be Cast OUT of them, including George Warmonger Bush, Little Dick Chicanery, Condoosleezee Rice Patty, Paul Wolfwits, Alan Greenspandex, Larry Edomite Silverstein, and any other Lying Conniving Edomites, who do not Quickly Write their Full Confessions in their Books, and Publish them on Amazon for everyone to Study, if they Want to, which also Includes the Lying Trumpeter who Livz in the Little White Outhouse, which has the 2 very Odious Holes for the Dimwitcrats and Reprobates to Squat on, which Stinks with Ancient Elephant Droppings and Fresh Political Donkey Dung from the Top to the Bottom, which is Full of Political and False Economic Farts, you might say, which Stink to the Highest Heaven, as Saint Peter might say; but, I would say that it Stinks to the Lowest Hell! †‡§§

11-10 [_] Well, my Friend, I would say that you pretty well Summed it all up, except that you left Out the Part about them having a CHOICE to go Liv in the Wilderness with the Snakes, Bears, Lions, Tigers, Wolves, Skunks, Porcupines, Scorpions, Spiders, Mice, Weasels, Groundhogs, Raccoons, Opossums, Prairie Dogs, Badgers, **Wolverines,** Bisons, Water Buffalos, Leopards, Panthers, Elephants, Giraffes, Elks, Deers, and whatever might Liv in the Wilderness of SIN! †§‡

— Chapter 12 —

The Conclusion!

12-01 [_] O Holy Moses, I Thot for Sure that you would be giving to us a Long List of Very Boring COMMANDMENTS to Learn and OBEY; but, you are only Asking for just ONE Thing, which is for us Education Slaves, Work Slaves, Tax Slaves, Insurance Slaves, Rent Slaves, Home-owner Slaves, Interest Slaves, Mortgage Slaves, ElecTrickery Bills Slaves, Food Bills Slaves, Water Bills Slaves, Gas Bills Slaves, Transportation Bills Slaves, Endless Repair Bills Slaves, Telephone Bills Slaves, Internet Bills Slaves, Entertainment Bills Slaves, Drug Bills Slaves, Dr. Pill Popper Bills Slaves, Dr. Niif Bills Slaves, Dr. Insanity Bills Slaves, Hospital Bills Slaves, Childcare Bills Slaves, Nursing Home Bills Slaves, Funeral Home Bills Slaves, Lawyer Bills Slaves, Rat Bills Slaves, Dog Bills Slaves, Cat Bills Slaves, Horse Bills Slaves, Cow Bills Slaves, Donkey Bills Slaves, and whatever other Kinds and Colors of SLAVES that People might be — all beCause of those Lying Conniving EDOMITES, who Set Up that Evil Slavery System of Satan, the DEVIL!‡

Ray,

It was devastating to learn of Congressman John Lewis'
passing last Friday. He was the best of us, a titan of civil rights,
and a true hero.

More than just the conscience of Congress, he was the
conscience of America. He always stood for what was right, no
matter the cost. During last year's impeachment hearings,
Rep. Lewis said: **"When you see something that is not
right, not just, not fair, you have a moral obligation to say
something, to do something."** Rep. Lewis embodied that
statement every day of his life, and we must do the same.

12-02 [_] O Holy Moses, you and your Selected King are no doubt the only Inspired Authors in all of World History, who have Justified Paragraphs in your 8.5 by 11-inch Editions of your Good Books, which makes them Unique among all Books in the Whole World, which should Upgrade the Value of them as Collector's Items: beCause you have NO Competitors, at all: beCause you 2 are the only Living INSPIRED AUTHORS. For Example, Mohammad never Wrote so much as one Sentence during his entire Life, whose Holy Koran has been Greatly Improved by your Selected King, in: **"The New MAGNIFIED Version of the HOLY KORAN!" (WHY MuhamMAD went to Hell for Spiritual MURDER!) By The Worldwide People's Revolution!®** Book 089, which is a Masterpiece of Fine Literature, once you get well into it. However, I just Received an E-mail Letter from Billionaire Tom Steyer, who Commented on the Life of Saint John Lewis, who was the Best of us, a Titan for Civil Rights, and a True American HERO, who was Awarded the Medal of Freedom, the Medal of Honor as a Civil Rights Champion, and several other Awards; but, he Failed to get a Condensed Version of: **"MARK TWAIN Races for the PRESIDENCY with a Landslide VICTORY!" (The 2020 Presidential Candidates Desperately Need Some STRONG Undefeatable COMPETITION!) By The Worldwide People's Revolution!®** Book 033B. Nevertheless, his Statement about having a

Moral Obligation to Do something to Correct the Evils of this World, is what is now Bothering my Conscience. †§‡

12-03 [_] Well, my Friend, if it Greatly Bothers your Conscience, why do you not Do what Jesus Christ said to Do, and go Sell ALL that you have, except for a large Comfortable VAN, and get yourself a Million or so Copies of this Inspired Book, and a Lover of Truths to Help you to Pass them Out for FREE in Sin City, to whomever Promises to REED them, whereby you will be Doing Humanity a Truly GREAT Favor, while also Guaranteeing yourself the very same Just Reward that will be Given by God to his Selected King, during the Judgment Day, when the Whole Truth is Revealed about all Important Subjects — that is, IF there is a Judgment Day, and any Rewards at all, which Require FAITH in them, if we have it; and I do not Expect very many People to have it; but, it only Requires just ONE Fairly Rich Man or Womb-man to have that Faith, whereby "VOTE for The GOAT!" (The New Political Party that has Guaranteed Solutions for our Massive Problems!) By The Worldwide People's Revolution!® Book 109, will be the Talk of the Town, as they say: beCause, it contains "Guaranteed Solutions!" (HOW to Solve our Local and Global Problems in the Most-Rational Manner Possible!) By The Worldwide People's Revolution!® Book 080, just like all of the other Inspired Books by our Selected King, who is having "the Time of his Life," as they say, Producing Inspired BOOKS, and many more Books than most People care to Reed: beCause, they have not had the Faith to Reed so much as ONE! §§

12-04 [_] ♥♦♦♦♦♦♦♦♥ O Holy Moses, after Thinking about it for a Considerable Amount of Time, I have Concluded that I am going to Accept your Good Advice, and go Sell ALL that I have, except for my New Van, which is about 20 feet Long, and will Contain at least 100 Boxes of these Books, if the Springs are Strong enough to Carry them, which I will Pass Out on the Streets of Sin City with my Sweet Wife, if I can Persuade her that it is a Good Idea, whose Time has Come: beCause, we are more than 60 Years Old, and once this Good News goes Out around the Whole Country, those Wooden / Plastic Firetrap Mouse-infested Cockroach Dens and Old Rusty Cars will not be Worth 2 Match Sticks and 2 Gallons of Gas: beCause, all Sane People will be Ready to DEPART from them, and Move into those "GLORIOUS Swanky Hotels Castles and Fortresses!" (Beautiful Planned City States for WISE Intelligent Well-Educated People with Common Sense and Good Understanding!) By The Worldwide People's Revolution!® Book 019B, which will Solve at least 5,000 of their Problems! Yes, that is the GOOD NEWS about it all; but, the Bad News is the DANGER that they will not Act WISELY, and DEMAND: "The GREAT Worldwide TELEVISED Court HEARING!" (That Great Meeting of the Most-Intelligent and Well-Educated Minds!) By The Worldwide People's Revolution!® Book 041B, whereby all of these Things can be Handled by Wise People, in a Civilized Manner, without Burning Down any Cities of Confusion, without any Ugly Riots, Protest Marches, nor Hateful WARS: beCause of Using our Heads to THINK and REMEMBER! Yes, Adolf Hitler only Asked for a Worldwide Radio DEBATE with the Leaders of France, Great Britain, Russia, and "The Divided States of United Lies!" (The so-called "United States of North America" in Disguise!) By The Worldwide People's Revolution!® Book 058, who Refused to Settle the Important Issues of that Time in a Peaceful Logical Manner, in a COURTROOM, with Just Judges in Charge of it, including German Judges, who have the same Civil RIGHTS as all Nations have, which Hearings should be Published in ALL Major Languages in ALL Major Nations, and Hopefully in ALL Minor Nations, whose People Need to Learn what is going on: beCause, the Oceans are RISING, and those Islanders might Need some Tall Strong Stone WALLS, just to Save themselves Alive!‡

12-05 [_] Well, my Friend, I must Agree with you, 100%, which is WHY that I Checked these Boxes [_] with LARGE GREEN-X Marks: beCause, I Know for a Fact that those Firetrap Houses will not be Worth even ONE Dollar for their Ashes, if they all Ascend Up to Heaven in Great Billowing Black Clouds of Highly-TOXIC SMOKE, just beCause some True NIGERZ Lost their Riit Miindz, and Decided to have a Great Year of JUBILEE without any Common Sense! §‡

12-06 [_] O Holy Moses, I may not be Able to Persuade my Fearful Wife that it is a Good Time to SELL OUT, while Real Estate Prices are Fairly Reasonable; but, I can Promise you that I will Skip a few Meals, just to put Copies of this Inspired Book into Mail Boxes, Legally, by Wearing my Face Mask, and going from Door to Door in some Strange City of Massive Confusion, where the Security Cameras will be Useless: beCause, I just Happen to have no less than 20 Cousins, who will be Happy to Help me to Distribute these Extremely Good Books, which are not Asking anyone to Say nor Do any Evil Things; but, only to DEMAND **"The GWTCH!"** Book 041B. †§‡

12-07 [_] †‡ Well, my Friend, if you have 20 Trustworthy Cousins, I suggest that you Distribute the less-expensive 8.5 by 11-inch Black and White Edition of this Inspired Book to all of them, who can Order a Colored Edition, if they Really Like it, and Give the B&W Edition to whomever might reed it, who can Do the same Thing, whereby you can easily Discover which ones of those Cousins are Trustworthy: beCause, only the Trustworthy ones will Order a Colored Edition, and also Skip a Meal or 2 of Dog Foods and/or Hog Slop, just to Buy the Book: beCause they Believe in FASTING and PRAYING, which is not a very BAD Thing to Do; but, it is a very GOOD Thing to Do, or else Moses, Elijah, King David, Isaiah, Jeremiah, Ezekiel, Joel, Jonah, Hosea, Amos, Jesus, John, Peter, James, and the Apostle Paul would not have been DOING IT! But, behold, they did more Fasting than any Men who ever Lived! Therefore, just how BAD could it be, my Friend?

12-08 [_] O Holy Moses, I am Fully Persuaded with the Apostle Paul that Fasting is a GOOD Thing; but, I simply do not have the Time for Doing it: beCause, I have to Maintain my JOB with Poor Old Uncle Jobe, who is Covered with Boils from his Itching Head to his Stinking Feet! †§‡§§

12-09 [_] Well, my Friend, I am Sure that God Simputhiizuz with you, and Understands the Situation at Hand: beCause he Knows all Things, including the Capitalist TRAP that you have Fallen Headlong into. Therefore, just Do whatever that you can Do to Help "The Worldwide People's Revolution!" (A Comprehensive Plan for Obtaining Worldwide Law, Order, Obedience, Peace and True Prosperity!) By The Worldwide People's Revolution!® Book 108, and God will Bless you with the same Just Reward that he will Bless the Remainder of us Believers. Yes, we are all in this Bottomless Pit of Massive Confusion, TOGETHER, with only ONE WAY OUT of it, which is to Cling to *the Rope of HOPE,* and Push and Pull on each other, until we Escape from it, by the Grace of GOD, who has Sent our Selected King with "Guaranteed Solutions!" (HOW to Solve our Local and Global Problems in the Most-Rational Manner Possible!) By The Worldwide People's Revolution!® Book 080: beCause, "All of the Arguments are in Favor of our Selected King, who has Zero Challengers!" (Before you Attend another Election Deception, you should Carefully Study this Inspired Book with an Honest Open Mind!) By The Worldwide People's Revolution!® Book 085, who has "The Swanky Sword of Divine Truths!" (The Most-Powerful Weapon in the Whole Universe!) By The Worldwide People's Revolution!® Book 067, which cannot be Defeated by any Election Deceptions: beCause, all Honest Americans are going to Reed this Inspired Book, and "VOTE for The GOAT!" (The New Political Party that has Guaranteed Solutions for our Massive Problems!) By The Worldwide People's Revolution!® Book 109. Yes, in Order to Do that, they only Need a single Sheet of Paper, or Postcard, upon which they can Write, in BIG **BOLD** Letters: **I VOTE FOR THE GOAT** — (Printed Name, Date, and Signature) and Mail that Postcard to: The Speaker of the House of Representatives, Capitol Hill, Washington, D.C. 20515-0001; but, not until at least October 15th, just to give to them enough Time to Conform to Reason and Logic, before: **"The Great ATOMIC NIGHTMARE!" (The Saddest Story in World History!) By The Great White Bald Eagle!** Book 099. Yes, if 200 Million Americans Send a *Vote for the Goat* Note to the Speaker of the House of Representatives, and she does not Humbly Submit to Reason and Logic, the Russians and Chinese have Agreed, in Secret, to make Washington and New Yuck City into Parking Lots for Submarines, if you know what I Mean: beCAUSE they are also getting SICK with the BUG-19, or some other Bug, which can easily be Eliminated by Constructing those **"GLORIOUS Swanky Hotels Castles and Fortresses!" (Beautiful Planned City States for WISE Intelligent Well-Educated People with Common Sense and Good Understanding!) By The Worldwide People's Revolution!**® Book 019B. However, if Americans do not have the Faith to Do that, they will Deserve to Suffer the Consequences of their own Stubbornness. †§‡§§

More than one way to skin a cat. ... There's more than one way to skin a cat means there are many ways to do something, there are many ways to achieve a goal. The oldest known use of the phrase dates back to 1854, in the work 'Way down East; or, Portraitures of Yankee Life by Seba Smith.

grammarist.com › phrase › more-than-one-way-to-skin... ▾
There's more than one way to skin a cat - Grammarist

Moody, in full Dwight Lyman Moody, (born February 5, 1837, East Northfield, Massachusetts, U.S.—died December 22, 1899, Northfield, Massachusetts), prominent American evangelist who set the pattern for later evangelism in large cities.

www.britannica.com › biography › Dwight-L-Moody ▾
Dwight L. Moody | Biography & Facts | Britannica

12-10 [_] O Holy Moses, I See that there is more than one Way to Skin the Cat, as they say, and I Promise to Do my Best to not Hurt that Cat in any Way, nor even Rub her Furry Hairs Backwards: beCause, I Know for a Fact that she is very MOODY, and is not a Distant Relative of Dwight L. Moody, who, along with the Fiery Billy Sunday and Dr. Rev. Billy Graham, would have been the First to get onto this Band Wagon, and Ride it Straight into HEAVEN, as Martyrs for the Cause, if it Required it! But, behold, no such Heroes are Needed, now that we have the Beloved Internet.

"White Lives Matter! Do not give to me any RFID Chip Shots."

{There is an Example of how to Build a 10,000-gallon Cistern without any Metal. Amazingly, none of the Tiles have Fallen Off, in spite of several Earthquakes! And it does not Leak. However, it did Require 6 Months for me to Build it, one Concrete Block at a Time.}

— Chapter 40 —

A Long List of other Fascinating Literature by the same Inspired Author

[_] 40-001 — "LIGHTNING **Versus the** Lightning Bug!" (HOW almost Everyone can become Moderately RICH, without Telling Any Lies nor Selling Any Capitalist Trash!) By The Worldwide People's Revolution!® Book 001B.

[_] 40-002 — "What is WRong with those Professing Christians?" (A Self-Examination of the Heart of the Body of Good Government!) By The Worldwide People's Revolution!® Book 002B.

[_] 40-003 — "For the Love of Money!" (The Strange Things that People Say and Do to Get more Money!) By The Worldwide People's Revolution!® Book 003B.

[_] 40-004 — "How Best to Prepare for CLIMATE CHANGES!" (The Wisest Plan for Mankind to Follow!) By The Worldwide People's Revolution!® Book 004B.

[_] 40-005 — "Why do I have to be Surrounded by CRAZY PEOPLE!" (Do almost all People Feel like they are Surrounded by CRAZY People?) By The Worldwide People's Revolution!® Book 005B.

[_] 40-006 — "The Washington Journal is a FARCE! (C-SPAN Managers are not very WISE!) By The Worldwide People's Revolution!® Book 006C. (This Book has lots of Good Humor.)

[_] 40-007 — "The PRAYERS of PUMPKINHEADS!" (This Book is otherwise known as the Prayers of Preachers, Priests, Professors, Politicians, Prostitutes, Policemen, Pumpkinheads, Punks, Prisoners, and other Professionals — in other Words, the Capital P People!) By The Worldwide People's Revolution!® Book 007B. (Some of it is for Adults only.)

[_] 40-008 — "A Sound Argument for Good Masters and Obedient Servants!" (WHY Everyone Needs a Good Master, and every

Master Needs Good Obedient Servants!) By The Worldwide People's Revolution!® Book 008B.

[_] 40-009 — "WHY are some Preachers so POOR?" (HOW almost all Preachers can Get Moderately RICH, without Preaching any Outlandish LIES!) By The Worldwide People's Revolution!® Book 009B.

[_] 40-010 — "GOOD NEWS for REBEL WOMEN!" (HOW almost all Wives can become Moderately RICH without Leaving their Homes! Guaranteed!) By The Worldwide People's Revolution!® Book 010B.

[_] 40-011 — "The Low Court of Supreme Injustices is Brought to Trial!" (Our Selected King Butts Heads with the United States Supreme Court, with or without their Black Robes of Hypocrisies and Lies!) By The Worldwide People's Revolution!® Book 011B. (This Inspired Book contains the Famous *Declaration of Interdependence,* which is a Must Read. It also contains the Correct Wording for the Placard on the Statue of Liberty.)

[_] 40-012 — "The Right Design for Living!" (A List of Great Advantages for Building Beautiful Planned City States!) By The Worldwide People's Revolution!® Book 012B. (This Book contains many Important Drawings, as well as HOW to Save hundreds of Trillions of Dollars by Building Swanky Fortresses, and Living in Peace within them. It is a Companion Book of Book 011B, which contains many more Great Advantages for Swanky Fortresses.)

[_] 40-013 — **"The Gospel According to The Worldwide People's Revolution!®" (The Good News from the Most Modern Perspective!)** See Book 077. (This Book contains the Famous Sermon of Jonah to the Ninevites, whereby 120,000 People Repented in Sackcloth and Ashes! Do not Miss Out on it. Not even the Rev. Dr. Billy Graham got 120,000 Converts during one Day!)

[_] 40-014 — **"Poverty Hunger Riots Strikes Police Brutalities Election Deceptions and Civil Wars!"** (The High Price that we Earthlings have Paid for Leaving the Good Land!) By The Worldwide People's Revolution!® Book 014B.

[_] 40-015 — **"Seven Great Armies of Working Soldiers!"** (HOW to Provide a Way for Everyone to WORK: so as to Eliminate Poverty,

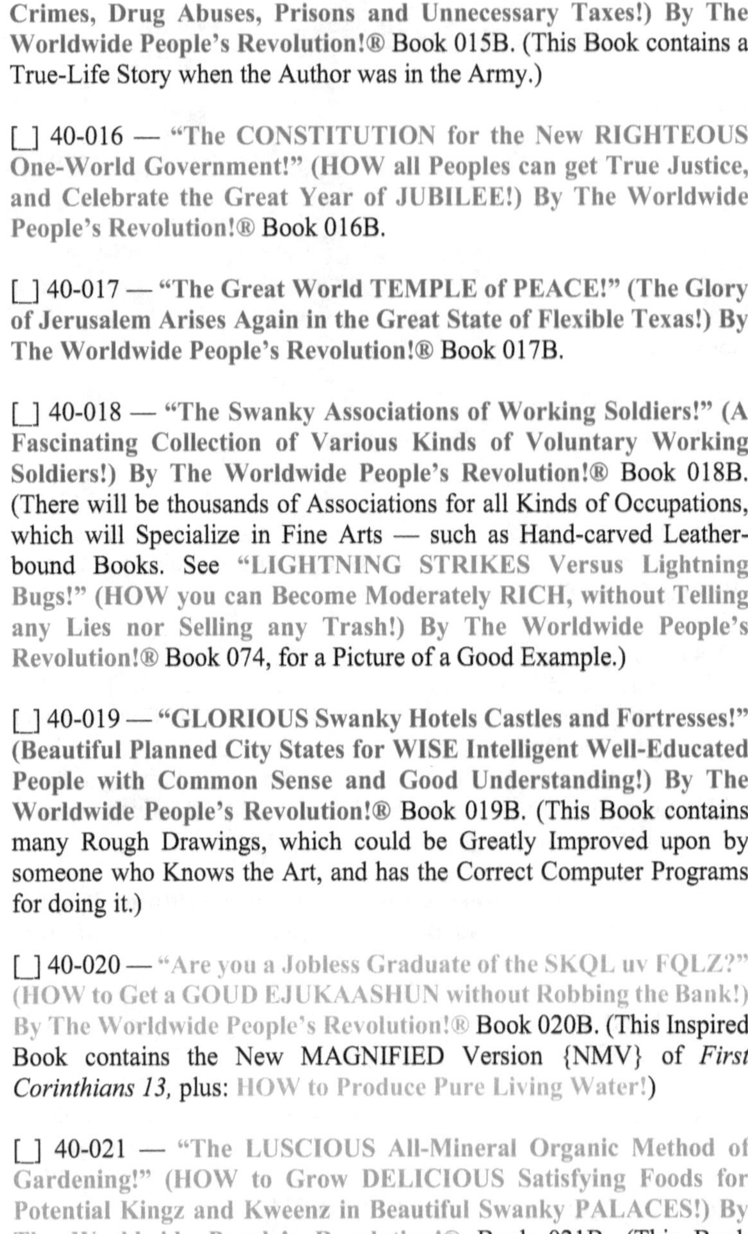

Crimes, Drug Abuses, Prisons and Unnecessary Taxes!) By The Worldwide People's Revolution!® Book 015B. (This Book contains a True-Life Story when the Author was in the Army.)

[_] 40-016 — "The CONSTITUTION for the New RIGHTEOUS One-World Government!" (HOW all Peoples can get True Justice, and Celebrate the Great Year of JUBILEE!) By The Worldwide People's Revolution!® Book 016B.

[_] 40-017 — "The Great World TEMPLE of PEACE!" (The Glory of Jerusalem Arises Again in the Great State of Flexible Texas!) By The Worldwide People's Revolution!® Book 017B.

[_] 40-018 — "The Swanky Associations of Working Soldiers!" (A Fascinating Collection of Various Kinds of Voluntary Working Soldiers!) By The Worldwide People's Revolution!® Book 018B. (There will be thousands of Associations for all Kinds of Occupations, which will Specialize in Fine Arts — such as Hand-carved Leather-bound Books. See "LIGHTNING STRIKES Versus Lightning Bugs!" (HOW you can Become Moderately RICH, without Telling any Lies nor Selling any Trash!) By The Worldwide People's Revolution!® Book 074, for a Picture of a Good Example.)

[_] 40-019 — "GLORIOUS Swanky Hotels Castles and Fortresses!" (Beautiful Planned City States for WISE Intelligent Well-Educated People with Common Sense and Good Understanding!) By The Worldwide People's Revolution!® Book 019B. (This Book contains many Rough Drawings, which could be Greatly Improved upon by someone who Knows the Art, and has the Correct Computer Programs for doing it.)

[_] 40-020 — "Are you a Jobless Graduate of the SKQL uv FQLZ?" (HOW to Get a GOUD EJUKAASHUN without Robbing the Bank!) By The Worldwide People's Revolution!® Book 020B. (This Inspired Book contains the New MAGNIFIED Version {NMV} of *First Corinthians 13*, plus: HOW to Produce Pure Living Water!)

[_] 40-021 — "The LUSCIOUS All-Mineral Organic Method of Gardening!" (HOW to Grow DELICIOUS Satisfying Foods for Potential Kingz and Kweenz in Beautiful Swanky PALACES!) By The Worldwide People's Revolution!® Book 021B. (This Book Explains HOW to make a Flood-proof Garden, while Trapping the Rainwater.)

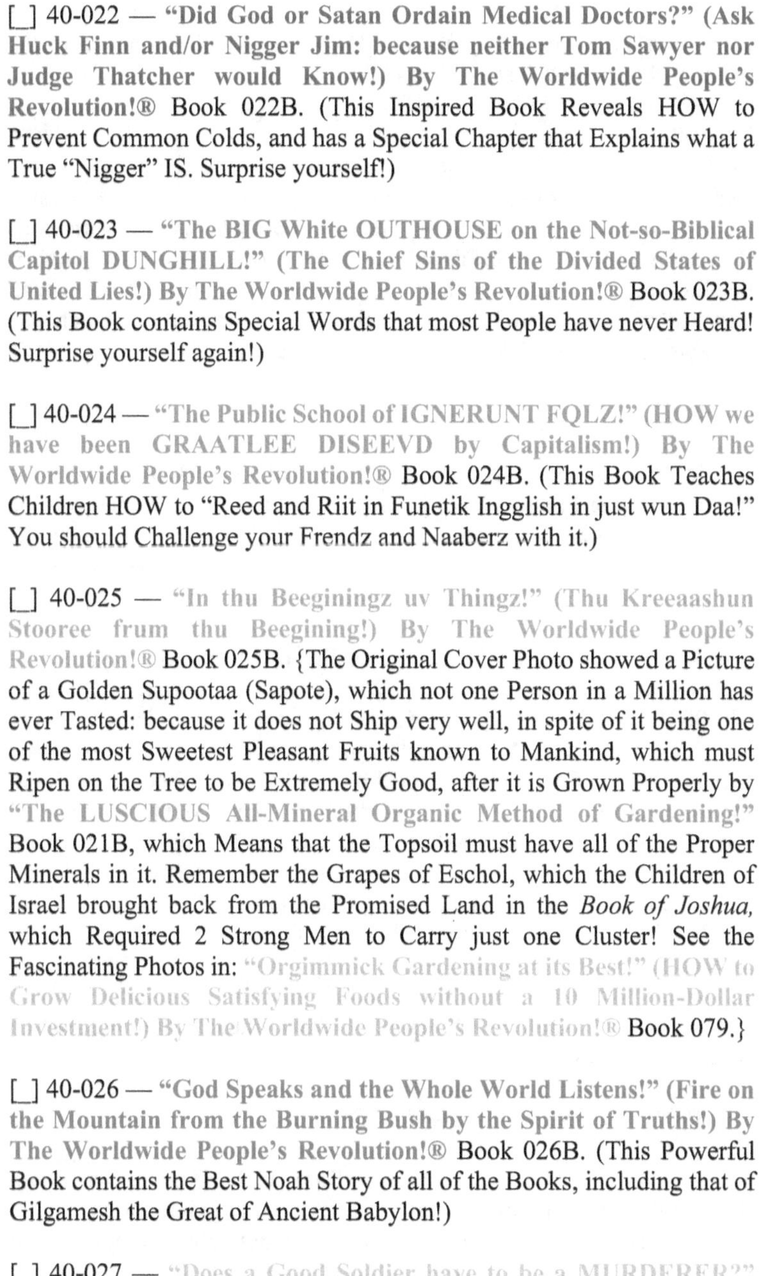

[_] 40-022 — "Did God or Satan Ordain Medical Doctors?" (Ask Huck Finn and/or Nigger Jim: because neither Tom Sawyer nor Judge Thatcher would Know!) By The Worldwide People's Revolution!® Book 022B. (This Inspired Book Reveals HOW to Prevent Common Colds, and has a Special Chapter that Explains what a True "Nigger" IS. Surprise yourself!)

[_] 40-023 — "The BIG White OUTHOUSE on the Not-so-Biblical Capitol DUNGHILL!" (The Chief Sins of the Divided States of United Lies!) By The Worldwide People's Revolution!® Book 023B. (This Book contains Special Words that most People have never Heard! Surprise yourself again!)

[_] 40-024 — "The Public School of IGNERUNT FQLZ!" (HOW we have been GRAATLEE DISEEVD by Capitalism!) By The Worldwide People's Revolution!® Book 024B. (This Book Teaches Children HOW to "Reed and Riit in Funetik Ingglish in just wun Daa!" You should Challenge your Frendz and Naaberz with it.)

[_] 40-025 — "In thu Beeginingz uv Thingz!" (Thu Kreeaashun Stooree frum thu Beegining!) By The Worldwide People's Revolution!® Book 025B. {The Original Cover Photo showed a Picture of a Golden Supootaa (Sapote), which not one Person in a Million has ever Tasted: because it does not Ship very well, in spite of it being one of the most Sweetest Pleasant Fruits known to Mankind, which must Ripen on the Tree to be Extremely Good, after it is Grown Properly by "The LUSCIOUS All-Mineral Organic Method of Gardening!" Book 021B, which Means that the Topsoil must have all of the Proper Minerals in it. Remember the Grapes of Eschol, which the Children of Israel brought back from the Promised Land in the *Book of Joshua,* which Required 2 Strong Men to Carry just one Cluster! See the Fascinating Photos in: "Orgimmick Gardening at its Best!" (HOW to Grow Delicious Satisfying Foods without a 10 Million-Dollar Investment!) By The Worldwide People's Revolution!® Book 079.}

[_] 40-026 — "God Speaks and the Whole World Listens!" (Fire on the Mountain from the Burning Bush by the Spirit of Truths!) By The Worldwide People's Revolution!® Book 026B. (This Powerful Book contains the Best Noah Story of all of the Books, including that of Gilgamesh the Great of Ancient Babylon!)

[_] 40-027 — "Does a Good Soldier have to be a MURDERER?" (Seven Great Swanky Armies of Voluntary Working Soldiers!) By

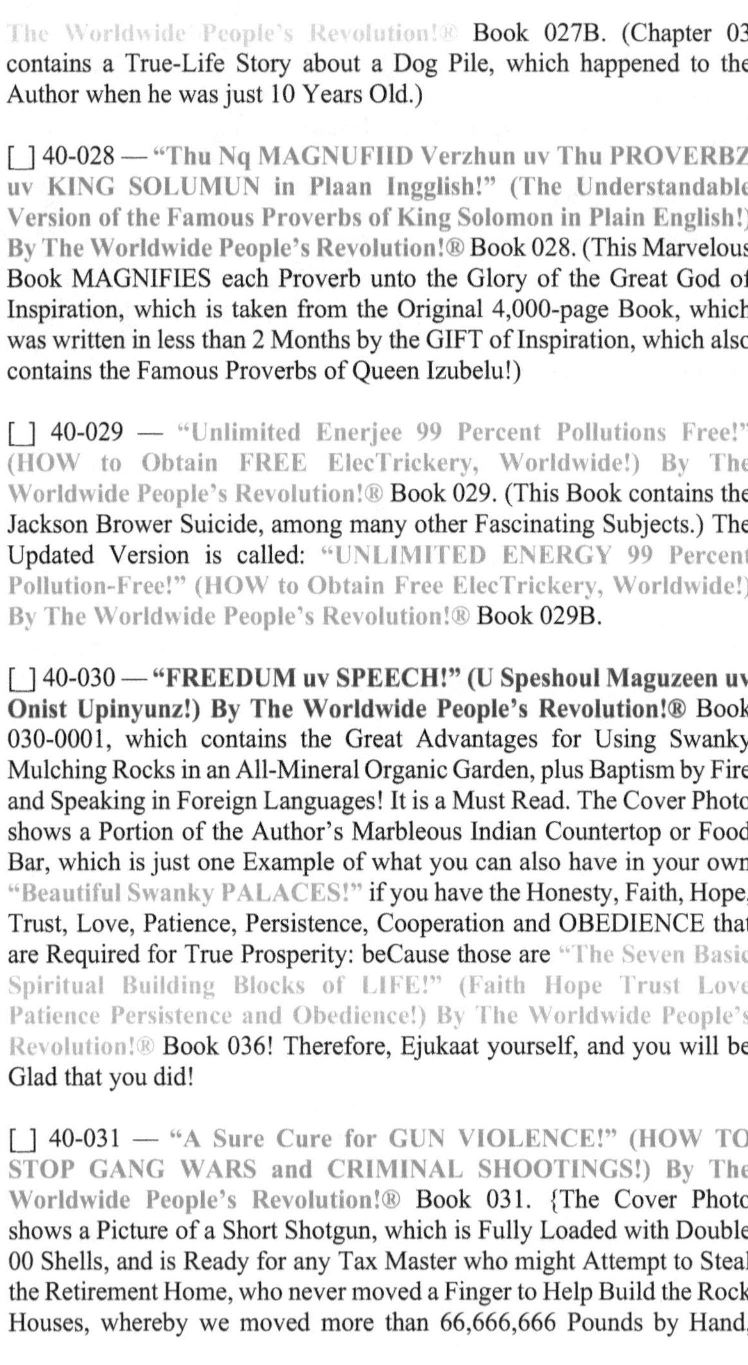

The Worldwide People's Revolution!® Book 027B. (Chapter 03 contains a True-Life Story about a Dog Pile, which happened to the Author when he was just 10 Years Old.)

[ ] 40-028 — "Thu Nq MAGNUFIID Verzhun uv Thu PROVERBZ uv KING SOLUMUN in Plaan Ingglish!" (The Understandable Version of the Famous Proverbs of King Solomon in Plain English!) By The Worldwide People's Revolution!® Book 028. (This Marvelous Book MAGNIFIES each Proverb unto the Glory of the Great God of Inspiration, which is taken from the Original 4,000-page Book, which was written in less than 2 Months by the GIFT of Inspiration, which also contains the Famous Proverbs of Queen Izubelu!)

[ ] 40-029 — "Unlimited Enerjee 99 Percent Pollutions Free!" (HOW to Obtain FREE ElecTrickery, Worldwide!) By The Worldwide People's Revolution!® Book 029. (This Book contains the Jackson Brower Suicide, among many other Fascinating Subjects.) The Updated Version is called: "UNLIMITED ENERGY 99 Percent Pollution-Free!" (HOW to Obtain Free ElecTrickery, Worldwide!) By The Worldwide People's Revolution!® Book 029B.

[ ] 40-030 — "FREEDUM uv SPEECH!" (U Speshoul Maguzeen uv Onist Upinyunz!) By The Worldwide People's Revolution!® Book 030-0001, which contains the Great Advantages for Using Swanky Mulching Rocks in an All-Mineral Organic Garden, plus Baptism by Fire and Speaking in Foreign Languages! It is a Must Read. The Cover Photo shows a Portion of the Author's Marbleous Indian Countertop or Food Bar, which is just one Example of what you can also have in your own "Beautiful Swanky PALACES!" if you have the Honesty, Faith, Hope, Trust, Love, Patience, Persistence, Cooperation and OBEDIENCE that are Required for True Prosperity: beCause those are "The Seven Basic Spiritual Building Blocks of LIFE!" (Faith Hope Trust Love Patience Persistence and Obedience!) By The Worldwide People's Revolution!® Book 036! Therefore, Ejukaat yourself, and you will be Glad that you did!

[ ] 40-031 — "A Sure Cure for GUN VIOLENCE!" (HOW TO STOP GANG WARS and CRIMINAL SHOOTINGS!) By The Worldwide People's Revolution!® Book 031. {The Cover Photo shows a Picture of a Short Shotgun, which is Fully Loaded with Double 00 Shells, and is Ready for any Tax Master who might Attempt to Steal the Retirement Home, who never moved a Finger to Help Build the Rock Houses, whereby we moved more than 66,666,666 Pounds by Hand,

whose Property was Cunningly Stolen by that False Anti-Christ WICKED Cover-up Government, which allowed Bankers to Rob us of 30 Years of Hard Labor and more than 300,000 dollars-worth of Investments in our Uncommon American Farm, which is Explained in: "LIGHTNING STRIKES Versus Lightning Bugs!" (HOW you can Become Moderately RICH, without Telling any Lies nor Selling any Trash!) By The Worldwide People's Revolution!® Book 074, which contains many Photographs with Profound Explanations! Do not be left out in the Darkness of Ignorance. Get Informed, now: beCause, **"The Great False Economy is now DEBUNKED!"** Book 053.}

[_] 40-032 — "AIIRMWVC and Reasonable Solutions!" (Aliens, Illegal Immigrants, Refugees, Migrant Workers and other Victims of Capitalism!) By The Worldwide People's Revolution!® Book 032. (This Inspired Book contains *the New MAGNIFIED Version of Job 33.*)

[_] 40-033 — "MARK TWAIN Races for the PRESIDENCY with a Landslide VICTORY!" (The 2020 Presidential Candidates Desperately Need Some STRONG Undefeatable COMPETITION!) By The Worldwide People's Revolution!® Book 033B. {This Book contains a Part of the Author's Autobiography, and his Personal Answers to the Questions in: "The Complete SURVEYS of our VALUES!" (SURVEYS of Religious Spiritual Political Governmental Sexual Social Moral Economic Business Labor Habitual and Miscellaneous VALUES!) Book 059. **The CONDENSED Version** is Book 033C, which most People Prefer.}

[_] 40-034 — "ECCLESIASTES Uncovered and Recovered!" (The New MAGNIFIED Version of Ecclesiastes and the Song of Solomon in Plain English!) By The Worldwide People's Revolution!® Book 034. (This is the Book that contains the Famous Sayings for *"There is a Time to be Born, and a Time to Die ..."* which has been Greatly Magnified!)

[_] 40-035 — "The Environmentalists' Perfect Paradise!" (HOW almost Everyone can be Living in a Beautiful Manmade Paradise!) By The Worldwide People's Revolution!® Book 035C. (This Book contains the NMV of *Psalm 48,* which will Amaze you, O Lady Doubtfulness!)

[_] 40-036 — "The Seven Basic Spiritual Building Blocks of LIFE!" (Faith Hope Trust Love Patience Persistence and Obedience!) By The Worldwide People's Revolution!® Book 036. (This Book contains the Mockingbird's Version of *Hebrews 11,* plus the NMV of *First Corinthians 13,* among many other "Goodies.")

[_] 40-037 — "DIETS!" (A Reasonable Solution for the "Eternal Controversy"!) By The Worldwide People's Revolution!® Book 037.

[_] 40-038 — "The Nature of CAPITALISM!" (A List of the EVILS of CAPITALISM!) By The Worldwide People's Revolution!® Book 038.

[_] 40-039 — "SWANGKEENOMIKS Rules the Roost!" (HOW all People can Prosper in a RIIT WAA, and STOP Polluting the Earth with Capitalist TRASH!) By The Worldwide People's Revolution!® Book 039. (The Cover Photo shows a Portion of the Author's Retirement Home, before the 5,000+ square-feet Concrete Roof was Installed, after moving more than 66 Million Pounds by Hand, and mostly by his own Boastful Hands!)

[_] 40-040 — "The New MAGNIFIED Version of The Book of MORMON!" (The Story of the White and Dark Indians in the Americas!) By Big Chief Standsover Bull in River of Life! Book 040, which comes in 2 Volumes of about 500 Pages, each. The Cover Photo on the First Volume shows the Queen of England's Golden Coach, and the Cover Photo on the Second Volume shows one of many Polished Spanish Marble Walls in our Selected King's Retirement Home, which is worth a thousand dollars per square yard, which is another Example of what you can also have, if you simply OBEY your Righteous KING! All such Marble is very Inspiring. No one could Study it for very long without Believing in a Great Creator God. The Picture does not do it Justice. You would have to See it in Person, and Wash it with Pure Water to bring Out the Beauty of it.

[_] 40-041 — "The GREAT Worldwide TELEVISED Court HEARING!" (That Great Meeting of the Most-Intelligent and Well-Educated Minds!) By The Worldwide People's Revolution!® Book 041B. {This is the Book that the World has long been Waiting for: beCause it will Overthrow the Evil Empires, and make it Possible to Establish "The New RIGHTEOUS One-World Government!" (HOW to Establish a Righteous One-World Government without Going to WAR!) By The Worldwide People's Revolution!® Book 056. This is the Greatest Idea since the Invention of the Light Bulb, Guaranteed!}

[_] 40-042 — "The Secret City of the Great King!" (HOW the True Church will Escape from the Great Tribulation!) By The Worldwide People's Revolution!® Book 042. (Be Sure to Inform your Friends, Relatives and Naaberz about this Wonderful Book: beCause they might also Want to Escape!)

[_] 40-043 — "Terrorists Beware that your Days are Numbered!" (HOW to Bring those Terrorist Attacks to a Screeching HALT!) By The Worldwide People's Revolution!® Book 043. (This Book also contains the Fascinating Book of LEHI, which has now been Restored!) †‡

[_] 40-044 — "The New MAGNIFIED Version of ISAIAH in Plain English!" (The Understandable Version of the Book of Isaiah!) By The Worldwide People's Revolution!® Book 044. (The Cover Photo shows a Swanky Potato and Avocado Salad with Sweet Peas and Corn, among other "Secret" Ingredients, which are Revealed within the Book. Remember that you can read many Words for Free in the Book Previews on www.Amazon.com.usa or UK.)

[_] 40-045 — "HOW to Become a HOLY Man!" (40 Good Reasons WHY People Should FAST and PRAY!) By The Worldwide People's Revolution!® Book 045, which is a Companion Book of:

[_] 40-046 — "The Proper RULES for FASTING!" (The Complete Instruction Manual for True Repentance!) By The Worldwide People's Revolution!® Book 046, which is a Companion Book of the above-mentioned Book, which contains a True-Life Story about an Old Black Mare called Lucy, who Fasted for 30 Days without Food nor Water, who was Physiologically "Born Again," as Jesus might say. See the Full Details in: "The New MAGNIFIED Version of The GOOD NEWS According to Saint JOHN!" (The Gospel According to Saint John Zebedee Boanerges in Plain English!) Book 062, which contains many Inspiring Photographs with Explanations!

[_] 40-047 — "Are Americans the Most-STUPID People who ever Lived?" (HOW Working People can PROSPER and Live in PEACE Under the Rulership of a RIGHTEOUS KING!) By The Worldwide People's Revolution!® Book 047. (The Cover Photo shows a large Portion of the Author's Living Room Floor, which is worth 100,000$, which is just another Good Example of what you can also have, just for Loving and Obeying your Elected King!)

[_] 40-048 — "An Amazing Collection of Wit and Wisdom!" (The Marvelous Tale of the Colorful Peacock from Angel Ridge, and the Strong Rope of Everlasting Hope!) By The Worldwide People's Revolution!® Book 048. (The Cover Photo shows a Book Display, which will be Greatly Enhanced during the Future, when all 364+ Inspired Books are on Display in a Swanky Truth-brary, as Opposed to the Public LIE-brary.)

[_] 40-049 — "Justifications for Capitalizations!" (WHY our Selected King DEFIES the School of FOOLS by Capitalizing LOVE and HATE!) By The Worldwide People's Revolution!® Book 049.

[_] 40-050 — "The END of CONFUSION!" (The Great CELEBRATION of the Magnificent Wedding of the Most-Humble, Honest Nations, and the Grand Year of JUBILEE!) By The Worldwide People's Revolution!® Book 050. (Just Try to Visualize those **"Seven Great Swanky Armies of Voluntary Working Soldiers"** Marching through the Valley of Megiddo, being Dressed in their Colorful Robes, while the Band Plays *The Battle Hymn of the Republic,* and the Choirs Sing the Praises of the Great KING of Kings! What a Sight and Sound that will be, which will be Climaxed in "The Great World TEMPLE of PEACE," when the Nations will get Married, along with our Elected King! Come one, come all to "The GREAT Worldwide TELEVISED Court HEARING," by Means of your Wide Flat-screen TVs, whereby you might Learn WHY, WHEN and HOW!) †‡

[_] 40-051 — "The Loathsome Burdens of the Independent Jackasses!" (A New Civilized Approach for Quietly Solving our Massive Problems!) By The Worldwide People's Revolution!® Book 051. (Just Think about the Multitude of almost Worthless Meetings of the Minds, who Strained themselves to Think of Reasonable Solutions for our Massive Problems, who sometimes even Prayed to God for Help; but, the Best Solutions have been here for no less than 40 Years — Thanks to the Spirit of Inspiration from GOD!)

[_] 40-052 — "Are we Tax Slaves of a Lower Order than those Lying Conniving EDOMITES!" (HOW to be Liberated From all Forms of Slavery, Worldwide!) By The Worldwide People's Revolution!® Book 052B. {This Inspired Book once had another Title and Author, which was not Acceptable by Amazon, which has now been Restored in all of its Glory, and is Published by more Trustworthy People, who are not Afraid of Controversies, nor of: "The Swanky Sword of Divine

Truths!" (The Most-Powerful Weapon in the Whole Universe!) By The Worldwide People's Revolution!® Book 067.}

[_] 40-053 — "The Great False Economy is now DEBUNKED!" (Adolf Hitler had a much Better Economic System!) By The Worldwide People's Revolution!® Book 053. {Trust me, Adolf was no Saint; but, during the Day of God's Judgment, he will be Justified, while his Anti-Christ Opponents will be Condemned: beCause they Refused to Attend a Worldwide Radio Debate with Adolf Hitler, whose Arguments will Stand Up during the Day of Judgment, which would have Prevented World War 2, and thus Saved the Lives of no less than 60 Million People! Likewise, we Tax Slaves must now Act more Wisely, and DEMAND "The GREAT Worldwide TELEVISED Court HEARING," Book 041B, whereby we might Save the World from that Dreadful Battle of Megiddo, called *Armageddon!* Yes, the Ball is now in YOUR Hands, O Potential Friend or Enemy, and you are now Responsible for it. Therefore, do not Shirk your Duty as a Free Citizen; but, Help us to Spread this Message, far and wide, whereby the Masses of People will be Demanding The GWTCH, and thus, Prevent "The Great ATOMIC NIGHTMARE!" (The Saddest Story in World History!) By The Great White Bald Eagle! Book 099.}

[_] 40-054 — "The UGLY Scarred Dishonest Face of Poor Old Miserable UNCLE SAM!" (A Memorial Day Legacy!) By The Worldwide People's Revolution!® Book 054. {NOTE: This Inspired Book was also Suppressed by Amazon, who will be most Ashamed of themselves if they do not Un-suppress it during the Future: beCause it will also be Published by People of Greater Faith, who Know for a Fact that it is the TRUTH! Therefore, just be Patient. Search for Book 054B, *King James Version.*}

[_] 40-055 — "The United States of the Whole World!" (A True Global Economy for the Masses of Working People!) By The Worldwide People's Revolution!® Book 055. (This Inspired Book contains many Colored Photographs with Explanations. It is a Good Book to Publish in Foreign Nations, who are not so Blinded by their Pride, who can See the Mountain of Lies much Better at a Distance from them: beCause of not being a Part of the American Corruption.) †‡

[_] 40-056 — "The New RIGHTEOUS One-World Government!" (HOW to Establish a Righteous One-World Government without Going to WAR!) By The Worldwide People's Revolution!® Book

056. (This is a KEY Book, which everyone should Study Carefully and Prayerfully.)

[_] 40-057 — "Those Ridiculous Contradictions within the Holy Bible!" (HOW to Read the Mutilated Bible with an Honest Open Mind!) By The Worldwide People's Revolution!® Book 057. {NOTE: Many Professing "Christians" Falsely Claim that their so-called *"Holy Bibles"* do not Contain any Contradictions, being "the Infallible Inspired Word of the Living God," but, without the Capitalized Words, and without Explaining just WHY there are more than 200 Contradictory Versions of it! This Book Reveals how to Deal with those Biblical Problems, and come to Understand WHY God Allowed it to Happen for the Truth's Sake. Trust God: beCause, you have never Heard this Explanation before now. See also: "C-SPAN-DEX!" (Your Filtered View of Bad Government!) By The Worldwide People's Revolution!® Book 097.}

[_] 40-058 — "The Divided States of United Lies!" (The so-called "United States of North America" in Disguise!) By The Worldwide People's Revolution!® Book 058. {NOTE: This is perhaps the most Referred to Book among all of the Books by our Selected King; but, that does not Mean that it is his Best Book by any Means, which is Well Camouflaged: so that it will Survive the Test of Time, even if the others are BURNED by the Anti-Christ Followers of Satan, who are Possession Worshipers of the Worst Kind, who Seek to Justify American Lies, rather than Quickly Confess them, and thus Escape from their Self-made Prison of Propagandish Lies! Just be Perfectly Honest, and you will have no Problem with any of our Literature.}

[_] 40-059 — "The Complete SURVEYS of our VALUES!" (SURVEYS of Religious Spiritual Political Governmental Sexual Social Moral Economical Business Labor Habitual and Miscellaneous VALUES!) By The Worldwide People's Revolution!® Book 059. {NOTE: According to our Selected King, every Potential Leader in the World must Fill Out and File those Surveys on the Internet for everyone to Study, whereby the Best People might be Elected by those Wise People who have also Filled Out the Simplistic Surveys of their own Values, whereby they will be Qualified to VOTE. Otherwise, they will not be Qualified to Vote, which will Eliminate a LOT of Wasted Money on Election Deceptions, while at the same Time it will Educate a lot of Ignorant People, who Desperately Need to Study that Inspired Book before Voting for another Dimwitcrat, Reprobate, or Independent Jackass!}

[_] 40-059B — "The Simplistic SURVEYS of our VALUES!" Book 059B. (The Cover Photo shows some Beautiful African Antelopes, who are Free with a Capital F.)

[_] 40-060 — "HOW to Get our PRIORITIES in ORDER!" (The Glories of Democracy; and, Does DEMON-ocracy have its Priorities in Order?) By The Worldwide People's Revolution!® Book 060. This Book will need to be Re-written by a Collective Group of Wise People, who will Contribute their True-Life Stories during the Future, when they Wake Up and come to their Right Senses with the Prodigal Son of *Luke 15*. See:

[_] 40-061 — "The New MAGNIFIED Version of The GOOD NEWS According to Saint LUKE!" (The Magnified Gospel of Saint Luke in Plain English!) By The Worldwide People's Revolution!® Book 061, which is by Far the Best Version of that Gospel on the Earth, which has no Rivals at all among the other 200+ Versions. Guaranteed!

[_] 40-062 — "The New MAGNIFIED Version of The GOOD NEWS According to Saint JOHN!" (The Gospel According to Saint John Zebedee Boanerges [pronounced Boo-an-er-jeez] in Plain English!) By The Worldwide People's Revolution!® Book 062, which also has no Rivals among all of the other Versions: beCause this is no Translation of anything; but, it is the Inspired Words of the Living God, which were Revealed by the Holy Spirit to our Selected King, who has not Died, yet.

[_] 40-063 — "The New MAGNIFIED Version of the Book of ACTS!" (The Understandable Version of the Acts of the Apostles in Plain English!) By The Worldwide People's Revolution!® Book 063. (This Inspired Book makes it Understandable WHY the Jews Hated the Apostles so much. You will have to Read it to Believe it.)

[_] 40-064 — "The New MAGNIFIED Version of the PSALMS of King David!" (The Understandable Version of the Famous Psalms in Plain English!) By The Worldwide People's Revolution!® Book 064. You will be Amazed!

[_] 40-065 — "A List of FAIR Swanky Wages!" (The Equitable Wage System!) By The Worldwide People's Revolution!® Book 065. (All Hardworking People will LOVE this Good Book! You will also, if you Study it Carefully.)

[_] 40-066 — "Beautiful Swanky PALACES!" (A New Concept in Living Habits — Swanky Palaces for Poor People!) By The Worldwide People's Revolution!® Book 066. (You have no Idea what a "Swanky Palace" IS, unless you have read this Unique Book, or another one that Describes those Palaces, and several of them do; but, this one has the Best Description. ENJOY!)

[_] 40-067 — "The Swanky Sword of Divine Truths!" (The Most-Powerful Weapon in the Whole Universe!) By The Worldwide People's Revolution!® Book 067. (The very Reason that our Selected King has no Rivals is beCause of the Swanky Sword of Divine Truths, which no one can Defeat by any Means. Therefore, you Need to have it on your own Side, whereby no one can Defeat your Arguments! Be Strong, be Brave, have Faith and put on the Whole Armor of GOD!)

[_] 40-068 — "Has your Life become Extremely Complicated?" (HOW to Live a SIMPLE Life!) By The Worldwide People's Revolution!® Book 068. (Many People are not even Aware of just how Complicated their Lives are, until suddenly they are ready to Commit Suicide! It is Best to Prevent all such Evil Things, and this Book tells HOW.)

[_] 40-069 — "The IDEAL Place to Live!" (HOW to Discover the Ideal Place to Live!) By The Worldwide People's Revolution!® Book 069. {NOTE: Our Selected King Searched the World over, and did not Discover any Idea Place to Live. Therefore, he Concluded that we must Make our own. Yes, we must Build those "GLORIOUS Swanky Hotels Castles and Fortresses!" (Beautiful Planned City States for WISE Intelligent Well-Educated People with Common Sense and Good Understanding!) By The Worldwide People's Revolution!® Book 019B, even if we must DRAFT "Seven Great Armies of Working Soldiers!" (HOW to Provide a Way for Everyone to WORK: so as to Eliminate Poverty, Crimes, Drug Abuses, Prisons and Unnecessary Taxes!) By The Worldwide People's Revolution!® Book 015B; and what on this Good Earth could Prove to be more Profitable than that, and without going to WAR?}

[_] 40-070 — "Our Elected King Who Speaks Out!" (It is High Time for some Sane Person to Get Control of this Insane World!) By The Worldwide People's Revolution!® Book 070. (This Inspired Book contains a Special Speech that is Addressed to both Houses of the Congress in Washington. You will Love it, O Honest Man of Greater Faith!)

[_] 40-071 — "How GAY is GOD?" (Oh, the Wonders of it all, when it ALL Hangs Out!) By The Worldwide People's Revolution!® Book 071. (Do not Judge the Book, until you have Carefully "Red" all of it. You will be Surprised by the Provable Truths within it, and Greatly Humored by the Author's Exceptionally Good Humor, who is less Gay than God, who has never had any Sexual Intercourse during his entire Life! In other Words, he is a VIRGIN!)

[_] 40-072 — "LIGHTNING STRIKES Versus Lightning Bugs and Impotent Fireflies!" (A Memorial Photo Album of some Real American Heroes!) By The Worldwide People's Revolution!® Book 072. (NOTE: This Book is Unique among all of the Books by our Selected King: beCause he did not get to Proof-read it before the Computer Crashed. It just Happened to be Saved on a Computer Chip before the Computer Crashed, and therefore it was Saved in PDF. But, the Corrections did not get made, which makes it a Special Collector's Item, which has more than 100 Colored Photos, which was what Caused the Crash.) †‡

[_] 40-073 — "The BEST of CAPITALISM!" (Corrections for: "LIGHTNING STRIKES Versus Lightning Bugs and Impotent Fireflies!") Book 073. (It is a completely new Book, except for those Corrections; and it is one of the Best Books in the World, which all Honest People will Love.)

[_] 40-074 — "LIGHTNING STRIKES Versus Lightning Bugs!" (HOW you can Become Moderately RICH, without Telling any Lies nor Selling any Trash!) By The Worldwide People's Revolution!® Book 074, which is the Perfection of all of the Lightning Striking Books, which is Recommended above all others for Mass Production: beCause it stands the Best Chance of being a Real Winner, just after this Book that you are now Reading, which has a Magnetizing Title!

[_] 40-075 — "What are the PUNISHMENTS for Dietary Sins?" (Have we Served ourselves Well at the Tables of our Lusts?) By The Worldwide People's Revolution!® Book 075. (This Book is too Controversial to be Published at this Time. Be very Patient until it is Available: beCause it is HOT!)

[_] 40-076 — "What is WRong with those CRAZY CHRISTIANS?" (A Self-Examination of the Heart of the Body of Good Government!) By The Worldwide People's Revolution!® Book 076.

[_] 40-077 — "The Gospel According to our Elected King!" (The Good News from the Most Modern Perspective!) By The Worldwide People's Revolution!® Book 077. (This is perhaps the Best Book that you will Discover on Amazon, which contains the Famous Sermon that Jonah gave to the Ninevites, plus a very Special Sermon by Jesus Christ, himself, which is taken from the Dead Sea Scrolls! It is simply a Marvelous Book that everyone must "Reed." ENJOY!) ‡

[_] 40-078 — "The Root Cause for almost all Evils!" (The Strange Things that People Say and Do to Get more Money!) By The Worldwide People's Revolution!® Book 078. (This Book contains many Colored Photographs with Fascinating Explanations!)

[_] 40-079 — "Orgimmick Gardening at its Best!" (HOW to Grow Delicious Satisfying Foods without a 10 Million-Dollar Investment!) By The Worldwide People's Revolution!® Book 079. (This Book also contains many Colored Photographs with Wonderful Explanations!)

[_] 40-080 — "Guaranteed Solutions!" (HOW to Solve our Local and Global Problems in the Most-Rational Manner Possible!) By The Worldwide People's Revolution!® Book 080. (See the Description on Amazon: because they Offer a ONE-MILLION-DOLLAR REWARD to anyone who can Prove our Selected King's Solutions to be WRong or Unworkable! Can you Beat that? Do you have all such Guaranteed Solutions? Does any Politician? Only our Selected King has those Provable Solutions: beCause God Blest him with them, which can be Proven in any Courtroom with Law and Order. ENJOY!)

[_] 40-081 — "Mexicans are more Intelligent than Americans!" (A Unique Challenge to all Americans and Mexicans!) By The Worldwide People's Revolution!® Book 081. {NOTE: The Remaining 275 Inspired Books by the Author of this Book may only be found in English, until we can get them Properly Translated into other Languages. Shame on you People who Killed him, who Broke his Heart with your Unbelief. May God have Mercy on your Poor Wretched Souls.} †§‡

[_] 40-081B — "¡Los Mexicanos son más Inteligentes que los Estadounidenses!" (¡Un Desafío Único para todos los Estadounidenses y Mexicanos!) By The Worldwide People's Revolution!® Book 082. {NOTA: Aquí está el primer Libro en Español, que puede no ser Perfecto; pero, es Perfectamente lo Suficientemente Bueno para Iluminar las Mentes de quien lo Estudia.}

[_] 40-082 — "The Process of Making a RIGHTEOUS KING!" (A Fascinating Autobiography of our Selected King!) By The Worldwide People's Revolution!® Book 082. {NOTE: He once had a 6,000-plus-page Autobiography, called: **"DIARRHEA of the Mind!"** which gave Details of his entire Life, since he was only 4 Years Old, when he had an Encounter with God, which has been Lost: beCause those Backup Disks became Obsolete, and were thus Trashed, along with the Obsolete Computer, which Costed 4,000-plus Dollars, along with the Hewlett-Packard Printer, which Costed another 4,000-plus Dollars, whose Antiquated Software would not Work with a Modern Computer, nor did Hewlett have an Updated Software Program for it: beCause they are Capitalist Scammers, who should be put Out of Business for Practicing Donald Trump Tactics! See: "The Nature of CAPITALISM!" (A List of the EVILS of CAPITALISM!) By The Worldwide People's Revolution!® Book 038.}

[_] 40-083 — "Was Billy Graham Greatly Deceived?" (Giving Honor to whom Honor is Due!) By The Worldwide People's Revolution!® Book 083. {NOTE: If you know a Grahamite, please Direct him or her to this Inspired Book, whereby he or she might be Converted to the Truths within it, and thus be Saved from Grahamite Perversions. Thank you in Advance. They will also Thank you for it: beCause they Suffer so Needlessly, when they should be Free, Healthy and Happy, like our Selected King, who has no Aches nor Pains, who used to Work Hard all Day long, and not be Weary, just like you can Reed in *the Book of Isaiah 40:31, NMV!*}

[_] 40-084 — "The New MAGNIFIED Version of the Book of DEUTERONOMY!" (The Understandable Version of Deuteronomy in Plain English!) Book 084. This is actually one of the Best Books within the entire Holy Bible, and also one of the Longest; but, do not allow that Fact to Deter you by any Means: beCause, "the Bigger Book is Normally a Better Book," which is True of a lot of Books, including all of the above Books: beCause it is the Nature of the Holy Spirit to get into Long-winded Sermons, you might say, which is WHY the Apostle Paul Preached until Midnight in *the Book of Acts,* until some Boy went to Sleep and Fell from a Window and Killed himself, whom the Apostle Paul Raised Up from the Dead and went on Preaching until the Dawn of the Day! And it is NOT Jewish Mythology! †§‡§§ {See: "The New MAGNIFIED Version of the Book of ACTS" for the Finest of Details, Book 063.}

[_] 40-085 — "All of the Arguments are in Favor of our Selected King, who has Zero Challengers!" (Before you Attend another Election Deception, you should Carefully Study this Inspired Book with an Honest Open Mind!) By The Worldwide People's Revolution!® Book 085.

[_] 40-086 — "Provable Truths that True Christians cannot Rightly Deny!" (A Fair Challenge for all Professing "Christians" to Meditate on with Honest Open Minds!) By The Worldwide People's Revolution!® Book 086.

[_] 40-087 — "How all Women can Get True Justice without Getting Divorced from God!" (The Unjust Case of Judge Brett Kavanaugh and Doctor Christine Blasey Ford is now Revisited by a Wise Son of King Solomon!) By The Worldwide People's Revolution!® B-087.

[_] 40-088 — "The New MAGNIFIED Version of GENESIS!" (The Enlightening Version of the Beginnings of Things!) By The Worldwide People's Revolution!® Book 088.

[_] 40-089 — "The New MAGNIFIED Version of the HOLY KORAN!" (WHY MuhamMAD went to Hell for Spiritual MURDER!) By The Worldwide People's Revolution!® Book 089. This is by Far the Best Version of the *Holy Koran,* which is Loved by all Honest Muslims, Hindus, Christians and Buddhists, Worldwide! Surprise yourself and others. Ask them what it Means? §‡

[_] 40-090 — "A New Jerusalem in the Great State of Flexible Texas!" (HOW to make Good Use of the Mississippi River!) By The Worldwide People's Revolution!® Book 090. This Book contains many Fascinating Photos of God's Handiwork. ENJOY!

[_] 40-091 — "What is The GREATEST SIN?" (And it is NOT Blasphemy Against the Holy Spirit!) By The Worldwide People's Revolution!® Book 091.

[_] 40-092 — "HOW to Make America (and all other Nations) Really GREAT Without Telling any LIES!" (The Founding Fathers would have Loved it!) By The Worldwide People's Revolution!® Book 092.

[_] 40-093 — "HOW Righteousness can Overcome Wickedness!" (The Triumph of the Soul who Knows God!) By The Enlightened Professor of Common Sense! Book 093. {Notice how the Calves in the

Cover Photo Segregated themselves by their Colors, from Left to Right. God Guided them. ‡}

[_] 40-094 — "Justifications for MAGNIFICATIONS!" (The Problem with Understanding a Complicated Contradictory Mutilated Unholy Bible!) Or: (The Problem with Inventing Lies that are too BIG to DIE!) By The Worldwide People's Revolution!® Book 094.

[_] 40-095 — "HOW to IDENTIFY God's Elected Ones!" (Are YOU one of the Elect?) By The Worldwide People's Revolution!® Book 095.

[_] 40-096 — "GOVERNMENT Versus Independence!" (How Much CONTROL Should a Government Have?") By The Worldwide People's Revolution!® Book 096.

[_] 40-097 — "C-SPAN-DEX!" (Your Filtered View of Bad Government!) By The Worldwide People's Revolution!® Book 097.

[_] 40-098 — "Profitable Swanky MULCHING ROCKS!" (30 Advantages for Using Swanky Mulching Rocks in an All-Mineral Organic Garden!) By The Worldwide People's Revolution!® Book 098. {Just Think, the School of Fools never Mentioned them, nor did the False Government, nor any of the False Churches: beCause they are Uneducated and Foolish.}

[_] 40-099 — "The Great ATOMIC NIGHTMARE!" (The Saddest Story in World History!) By The Great White Bald Eagle! Book 099. {NOTE: Let us Hope and Pray that no one ever has to Write this Book; but, if they Do, it should Spook the Devil Out of you!}

[_] 40-100 — "Our Selected King SPEAKS OUT!" (It is High Time for some Sane Person to get Total Control of this Insane World!) By The Worldwide People's Revolution!® Book 100!

[_] 40-101 — "What will you Do when the Rain STOPS?" (God's Last Resort to Save Mankind from his MADNESS!) By The Worldwide People's Revolution!® Book 101!

[_] 40-102 — "Beautiful Swanky Stone Dome Home COMPLEXES!" (HOW to Build SECURE Tax-proof, Insurance-proof, Self-air-conditioned, Paint-proof, Rot-proof, Termite-proof, Mouse-proof, Fireproof, Tornado-proof, Hurricane-proof, Thief-proof, and BOMB-PROOF Houses!) By The Worldwide People's Revolution!® Book 102.

[_] 40-103 — "Royal Swanky Buffets!" (The Best Feasts in the Whole World!) By The Worldwide People's Revolution!® Book 103.

[_] 40-104 — "101 Good Reasons and Great Advantages for Establishing a Righteous One-World Government!" (Government By the People, Of the People, and For the People!) By The Worldwide People's Revolution!® Book 104. This Book Suggests thousands of Good Reasons and Great Advantages. But, of course, you have to be Able to THINK, which seems to be something that Wicked Politicians cannot Do, or Refuse to Do; and neither can most Preachers and Teachers Do it. Therefore, this Inspired Book will Help them to Think and Remember.

[_] 40-105 — "The New MAGNIFIED Version of the Book of REVELATION!" (The Understandable Version of the Most-Controversial Book in the Whole World!) By The Worldwide People's Revolution!® Book 105. This Proverbial "Bombshell" will be Published just before the Second Coming of Jesus Christ! Get your Seatbelts Fastened! Be Prepared for Radical Changes!

[_] 40-106 — "The Naked Glory of Beautiful Mankind!" (1,000 Pages of Sheer Artistic BEAUTY!) By The Worldwide People's Revolution!® Book 106. (See Book 014B-02-09-T for the Explanation.)

[_] 40-107 — "The Beautiful Faces of Holy Men!" (The very Best that God has to Offer!) By The Worldwide People's Revolution!® Book 107.

[_] 40-108 — "The Worldwide People's Revolution!" (A Comprehensive Plan for Obtaining Worldwide Law, Order, Obedience, Peace and True Prosperity!) By The Worldwide People's Revolution!® Book 108.

[_] 40-109 — "VOTE for The GOAT!" (The New Political Party that has Guaranteed Solutions for our Massive Problems!) By The Worldwide People's Revolution!® Book 109.

[_] 40-110 — "IMPORTANT THINGS that Should Have Been Written in the Holy Bible!" (A Special Challenge to all Professing Christians, Jews, Hindus, Muslims and Atheists!) **By** The Irreverent Penname Scumbag! Book 110.

[_] 40-111 — "Hosts of HOAXES Live In Under Around and Over the Little White OUTHOUSE!" (WHY Spiritually-Blind Cowardly-Americans are Hunkering Down in their Empty Root Cellars!) **By** The Irreverent Penname Oversight! Book 111.

[_] 40-112 — "Should Wives Obey their Husbands?" (OR, Should Husbands OBEY their Wives?) **By** The Irreverent Penname Mockingbird! Book 112.

[_] 40-113 — "Modern Deceived SLAVES!" (10 Simple Steps for Liberating ALL Modern Slaves, Worldwide, Including Yourself!) **By** Liberty and Justice for ALL! Book 113.

[_] 40-114 — "Are you a Jobless Graduate of the School of Fools?" (How to Obtain a Good Education without Robbing the Bank, Selling any Trash, nor Telling any Lies!) **By** The Professor Wordcraft Enlightenment! Book 114.

[_] 40-115 — "Beautiful Swanky FASTING SANITARIUMS!" (HOW to Learn Good Self-Discipline!) **By** The Worldwide People's Revolution!® Book 115.

[_] 40-116 — "Swanky Institutions for Compassionate Corrections!" (How to Correct even the Most-Stubborn Bullies!) **By** The Biggest Bully of All Bullies! Book 116.

[_] 40-117 — "What is True PROGRESS???" (Are we Making any True Progress, at all?) **By** The Worldwide People's Revolution!® Book 117.

[_] 40-118 — "Is America a White Nation with a Black Heart?" (How to Separate Truth from Fiction!) **By** The Good Pastor of Uncommon Sense! Book 118.

[_] 40-119 — "Which Church is the Right Church?" (Can all Churches be Correct?) **By** The Good Pastor of Uncommon Sense! Book 119.

[_] 40-120 — "Do People Go to Heaven when they Die?" (The Unbelievable Truth about Life and Death!) **By The Good Pastor of Uncommon Sense!** Book 120.

[_] 40-121 — "The Hopeless Church of Little Faith!" (The Unholy Church of Graceful Sinners, who are Mostly just Liars and Hypocrites!) **By The Good Pastor of Uncommon Sense!** Book 121.

[_] 40-122 — "HOW to Make Proper REPARATIONS!" (True Justice for Black and White People, and Everyone in Between them!) **By The Worldwide People's Revolution!®** Book 122. (This Book was Inspired by: https://youtu.be/QOPGpE-sXh0 The Truth about the Confederacy in the United States | Full Version.)

[_] 40-123 — "What would Moses and Jesus Do with the Statues and Monuments???" (A Unique Plan for Solving the Problem, which Everyone can be Extra Happy with!) **By Liberty and Justice is for ALL!** Book 123.

[_] 40-124 — "Belgiculture!" (A Complete Master Plan for Solving the Countless Problems of Mankind!) **By The Worldwide People's Revolution!®** Belgique Book 124.

[_] 40-125 — "Good Lessons for Honest Wise Men!" (A Simplistic Plan for Totally Solving the Complicated Problems of Deceived Mankind!) **By The Smarter Professor of Common Sense!** Book 125.

[_] 40-126 — "The Sixth Book of Moses called GOOD GOVERNMENT!" (The Primary Missing Book in the Holy Bible!) **By The Worldwide People's Revolution!®** Book 126.

{NOTE: That List of Available Books will be Updated, Periodically, if we do not get Killed by some Thugs, who Work for those Lying Conniving Edomites!}